out of print
£9-00

1A15

RAIL CENTRES:
YORK

RAIL CENTRES:
YORK

K. HOOLE

LONDON

IAN ALLAN LTD

First published 1983

ISBN 0 7110 1320 9

© Ian Allan Ltd 1983

Published by Ian Allan Ltd, Shepperton, Surrey;
and printed by Ian Allan Printing Ltd at their works
at Coombelands in Runnymede, England

Contents

WHEREAS the making of a Railway from the City of York to and into the Township of Altofts, and the making of several branches from the said Railway, all within the West Riding of the County of York or County of the same City, would be of public Advantage, by opening additional and expeditious Communications between the City of York and various Parts of the said West Riding, and also of the East Riding of the said County of York, and might also be the Means ultimately of effectuating or facilitating the Establishment of a general expeditious line of Communication between the Northern Counties and the Midland and Western Parts of England and the Metropolis.

(Preamble to the York & North Midland Railway Act 21 June 1836)

Foreword

We have come a long way from the days of George Hudson whom posterity will remember as the 'Railway King'. His drive, initiative, and unorthodox — even dubious! — business methods ensured that York well and truly secured a place of lasting importance in the developing railway network. The growth of railways continued throughout the 19th century and in 1854 even the Hudson 'Empire' was swallowed up in an amalgamation out of which emerged the North Eastern Railway. This benevolent monopoly became one of the most progressive, influential, and financially strong companies in the country. The old North Eastern like to do things on a grand scale. The present York station, which celebrated its centenary in 1977, proudly stands as a memorial both to this great railway company and our Victorian forebears who boldly designed and engineered it.

Railways first came to York in 1839 and the unfolding story of their development has a fascination of its own. There are many varied facets. Here one can still see impressive buildings which formed part of the 1841 'old station', and gaze upon the architectural merits of the 1906 Headquarters Offices which housed the North Eastern's managerial and administrative heart. Then there is the 1877 station with its lofty curved roof where all the latest hardware of a busy modern railway system can be seen in action set against a 19th century backcloth.

The expansion, change and decline of a once extensive network of marshalling yards, locomotive sheds and workshops, forms yet another part of York's railway story. We have moved right through the steam era to the Inter City 125 trains; from primitive carriages to the luxury on wheels which we now accept as commonplace, and from the oil lamp to the latest signalling technology. York has all the ingredients of a thriving modern railway centre and there is always something of interest to be seen. Nor has York forgotten its links with the earlier railways for here we can recreate the glories of the past in the National Railway Museum.

As British Rail's first Area Manager in York from 1970 until moving on quite recently to the position of Operations Officer in the Leeds Division, I was the direct successor to past generations of distinguished officials who proudly bore the title of 'Station Master York'. Being possessed of more than a passing interest in matters historical, it was with great pleasure that I accepted Ken Hoole's invitation to pen a foreword to his latest book on one of my favourite topics. In fact I tend to look upon him as being the logical successor to that earlier historian William Weaver Tomlinson whose treatise on North Eastern history, first published in 1914, is still regarded as the standard text book.

As with many good stories, there remains a further chapter still to be written. We live in an era of ever increasing change and already the diverted East Coast main line which avoids the new Selby Coalfield is taking shape in readiness for opening during 1983. Hopefully we also look forward to electrification of the former North Eastern main line and towards ultimate realisation of the goal which that visionary Sir Vincent Raven — the North Eastern's last Chief Mechanical Engineer — so strongly advocated over 60 years ago.

York always was, still is and will continue to be a railway centre of significant interest. This book ably portrays the story of change since 1839. Long may York and its railways prosper!

K. C. Appleby
September 1982

Outline History

For centuries York has been a major centre of communications. In Roman times it was of great importance, with roads running north to south and east to west crossing at Eboracum, the Roman name for the city. Water transport on the Ouse and Foss played its part, and the stage coaches on the roads necessitated numerous coaching inns in the city. The coming of the railway in 1839 was the start of a close association which has lasted ever since as the city has successively been the headquarters of the York & North Midland Railway, North Eastern Railway, North Eastern Area of the LNER, North Eastern Region of British Railways, and now the enlarged Eastern Region, which absorbed the North Eastern Region in 1967.

The early history of the railways of York is dominated by a notable character, George Hudson, the driving force behind many early railways, who cut his teeth on the York & North Midland. His unethical financial dealings led to his downfall in 1849, but he lived until 1871, although never again a force in the railway field. Many of the lines in north-eastern England owed their inception and growth to Hudson, but more tangible remains came from the hand of his favourite architect, George Townsend Andrews, who received numerous commissions to design stations in Yorkshire and County Durham, many of which remain in use to this day, although not always for railway purposes.

Following Hudson came such men as George Leeman, H. S. Thompson, Henry Tennant, George Gibb, R. L. Wedgwood, and many others, who all left their mark during their sojourn at York. As the headquarters of the North Eastern Railway and its successors the railway staff played a large part in the life and development of the city, many of them attaining the highest offices of Lord Mayor and Sheriff.

Unfortunately in 1967, after 113 years, the words North Eastern disappeared from the title of the railways based at York, but the decision to site the headquarters of the new enlarged Eastern Region at York ensured a continuity of the city as a major railway administration and operations centre.

During its life York had only two permanent stations — one opened in 1841 and operated jointly by the York & North Midland and Great North of England companies, with the Great Northern as a regular visitor after the route to the south via Knottingley was opened in 1850, and the new station opened in 1877, with its lengthy platforms and magnificent curved roof. The centenary of the latter station was marked in 1977 by a display of old and new locomotives and coaches.

The motive power has changed, the method of signalling has changed, but railways still rely on the human element to operate successfully and safely, so that York still plays a large part in the railway of today. But York's railway buildings are not only offices as there are many other railway structures of interest, ranging from George Hudson's house to water towers, bridges, a garage, a laundry, a statue and a war memorial. Even York Cemetery has connections with the times when the city's railway system was new, for there can be found the graves of G. T. Andrews and his contemporaries whose names crop up time and time again in the reports of those early days. George Hudson was buried at Scrayingham, a village outside York and not far from Howsham, where he was born.

During his railway career one of Hudson's main objectives was to complete a line of railway from London to Edinburgh, as mentioned in the Y&NM Preamble, but he did not remain in office long enough to see his dream fulfilled. However, before he died the East Coast main line was growing in importance, and has continued to do so, forming one of the two main links between England and Scotland, with some of the modern trains covering the 393 miles between the two capitals in 285 minutes.

Right: **Rail routes to York.**

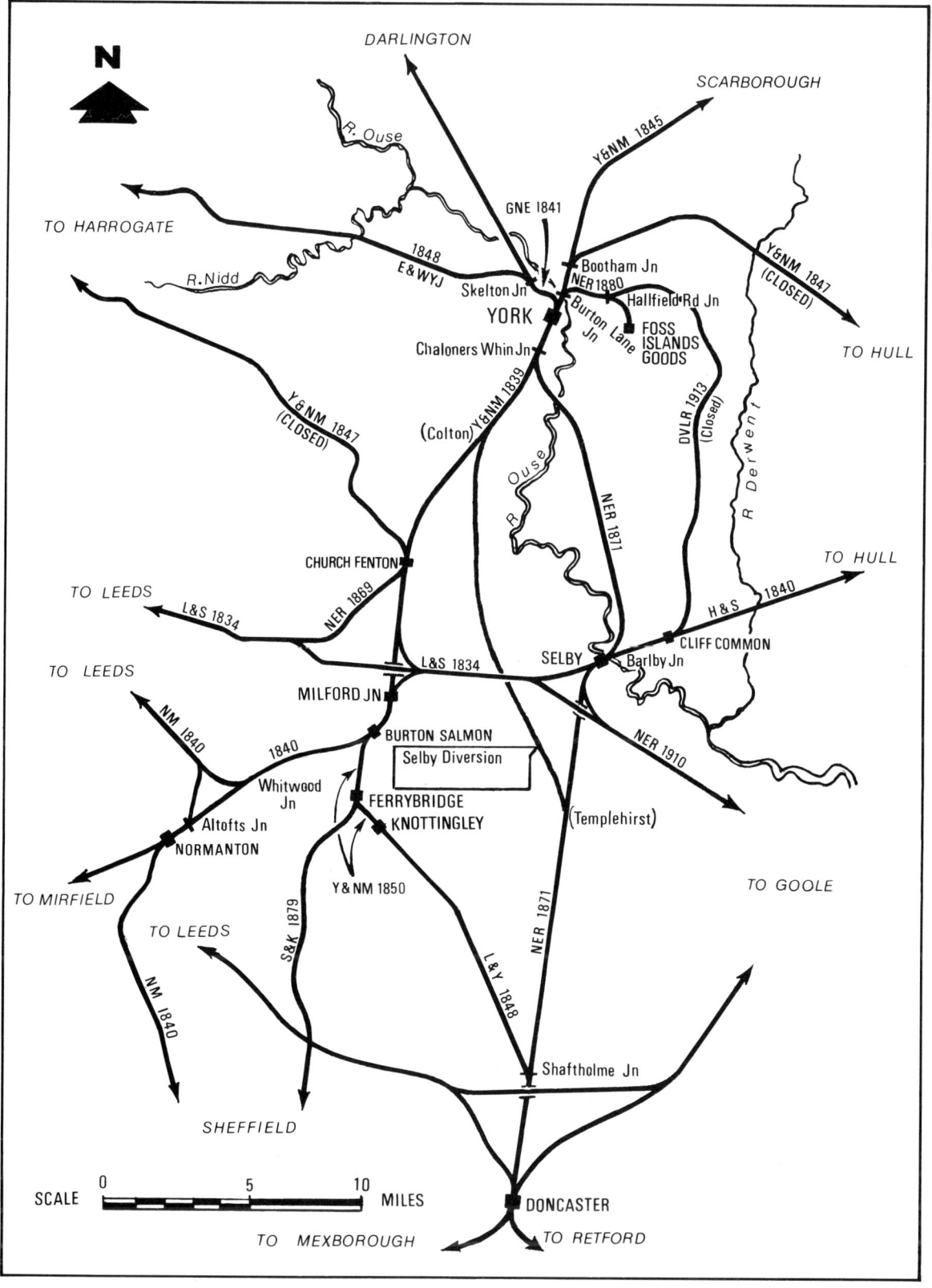

The opening of the Stockton & Darlington Railway — the world's first steam worked public railway — in September 1825, led to the citizens of towns in the north-east giving thought as to how their town could be served by a railway. The historic City of York was no exception and as early as 1826 a line northwards to join the Stockton & Darlington's Croft branch was suggested. Discussions went on for years but the formation of the Leeds & Selby Railway in 1830 focused attention on a line from York to Leeds. However, even then London was the objective of many of those supporting a railway to the south of York, but how to finance and build the intervening 188 miles of railway was the problem.

In 1833 a meeting was held in York to discuss the proposed railway to serve the city, although at that time there was no definite objective; fortuitously this was largely solved in 1835 with the formation of the North Midland Railway to build a line from Leeds to Derby, and by building a line from York to Normanton, to connect with the North Midland, a route to the south could be opened up. To take advantage of this the York & North Midland Railway was formed and this company was fortunate in that on its way to Normanton it had to cross the Leeds & Selby, where connections could be given to east and west.

The North Midland had access to London (Euston Square) over the Midland Counties (Derby-Rugby), or the Birmingham & Derby, and the London & Birmingham. Incidentally the North Midland, Midland Counties, and Birmingham & Derby companies amalgamated in 1844 to form the Midland Railway — a company which later had very close connections with the North Eastern, until both ceased to exist under the Grouping of 1923.

The York & North Midland was actually formed at a meeting held in York Guildhall on 13 October 1835, with the stated object of building a line from York to Normanton, and the scheme was so well supported that within 24 hours 75% of the £200,000 capital (in £50 shares) was taken up. A York draper, George Hudson, was appointed the company's first Chairman, and George Stephenson was appointed Engineer; he surveyed a route via Bolton Percy, Church Fenton and Castleford, missing Tadcaster which for years had been on the suggested route. Application was made to Parliament and on 21 June 1836 the company received its Act authorising a line from York to join the North Midland at Altofts, ¾ mile north of Normanton, with a branch from Whitwood to Methley to give access to Leeds (Hunslet

Above: A portrait of George Hudson (1800-1871), the 'Railway King', who was Chairman of the York & North Midland Railway when the first railway serving York was opened in 1839. He lived at 44 Monkgate, in a house which is still in existence. *Author's collection*

Above right: The site of the temporary Y&NM station outside the Walls, in use from 29 May 1839 to 4 January 1841, photographed in 1939 to mark the centenary of the opening of the line. The south end of the 1877 station can be seen on the left, with the wall of the former No 1 Erecting Shop of the Locomotive Works on the right. Across the centre of the photograph is Queen Street bridge, with the City Walls behind. The semaphore signal protected a level crossing giving road access to the Signal Engineer's Stores just inside the Walls. *BR*

Lane) over the North Midland, three curves to the Leeds & Selby at Milford, and an extension to reach the River Ouse at York.

Work on staking out the line commenced in September 1836, and in February 1837 tenders

were invited for the construction of the first $3\frac{1}{4}$ miles of line from York to Copmanthorpe; tenders for the subsequent lengths were accepted as the line progressed, the first objective being to join the Leeds & Selby at Milford.

In the same session of Parliament the Great North of England Railway received an Act to build a line from Gateshead to Croft (near Darlington) as part of a scheme for a line from Gateshead to York. The Act for the southern section was obtained in July 1837 and the line was based on the experience gained by the Stockton & Darlington Railway. At first the GNE had planned to make for Tadcaster rather than York and it needed some persuasion by the Y&NM Directors to make York the goal. In fact in September 1836 the Chairman and Directors of the Y&NM, accompanied by the Lord Mayor of York, waited on the GNE Directors 'to remonstrate with them respecting their intention of taking their line south by way of Tadcaster, in preference to this City'. The Y&NM went so far as to instruct Stephenson to

carry out an immediate survey from York to Croft so as to be in a position to oppose the GNE Bill if it persisted in by-passing York. In the event the GNE decided it would be more prudent to make for York, as confirmed by the 1837 Act. By September 1837 the GNE was inviting tenders for the section south of Croft and thus railways north and south of York were under construction simultaneously, with the Y&NM having a few months lead and less distance to cover.

Although the York & North Midland's consulting engineer, George Stephenson, had recommended that the terminus at York should be built outside the City Walls the 1836 Act allowed the line to 'commence at or near a certain garden or parcel of land' inside the Walls to the north of Tanner Row, where part of the site was taken up by a garden, dwelling house and tenement owned by Lady Hewley's Charity, with the garden and house leased to Thomas and James Backhouse. On another part, again owned by the Charity, was a Hospital for Women, and a third plot was taken up

Above left: **A fine drawing of the 1841 station, probably by the architect G. T. Andrews, recently purchased by the Friends of the National Railway Museum and presented to the NRM. This is believed to be the first time this drawing has been published. The office block was subsequently extended at each end and an additional storey added.**
Crown Copyright, National Railway Museum, York

Left: **If this view is compared with the previous illustration the extent of the additions can be seen, comprising the block nearest the camera and the whole of the top floor. The new office block, Hudson House, was under construction when this view was taken in April 1968.** *BR*

Above: **In 1906 a magnificent new office block for the NER Headquarters' staff was erected facing the end of the Old Station and the 1853 hotel. The Old Station frontage is on the left, with the 1906 offices in the background. Both buildings have since been cleaned and once again can be seen in their pristine condition.** *BR*

by the House of Correction. However, it was not until August 1838 that the Y&NM decided to build its station on this site provided it could be purchased at a reasonable price.

Because of progress with the line, and lack of progress with the site negotiations, it was decided in November 1838 that a station should be erected outside the walls in readiness for the opening of the line and the Engineer, Mr Cabry, was ins-

tructed to erect a temporary station which, so a contemporary account informs us, was built of wood and had two rooms, one for the company's secretary and the other for the booking clerk.

In the meantime negotiations had been proceeding with the GNE regarding the joint station and on 4 December 1838, on the occasion of a meeting between the two parties at Thirsk, a formal agreement was signed. To reach the station it was necessary to make an arch through the City Walls, and on 7 February 1839 three tenders for the work were considered: these ranged from £2,000 to £3,700 but the amounts were thought to be excessive and it was decided that the Y&NM should build the arch itself, with the work supervised by the architect, G. T. Andrews, whose design had been chosen in preference to that of Thomas Cabry, the company's engineer. Work went ahead so quickly that by the beginning of June 1839 the workmen were rapidly restoring the promenade over the arch spanning the route into the station and on 13 July the footpath was reopened: this walk along the crest of the walls is popular still, giving excellent views of many historic features of York and, particularly in this stretch, of the old station site, now partly occupied by the Eastern Region's Hudson House office block.

The first section of the York & North Midland Railway, from York to join the Leeds & Selby at Milford, was formally opened on 29 May 1839, with the public opening taking place on the following day. The trains gave connections to

Above left: An engraving of the 1841 station published in 1861. The viewpoint is above the 1839 arch through the City Walls, from the footpath that is still a popular walk today. The white building is the 1853 hotel, with the Minster behind. The additional bays built to serve the Scarborough trains are on the extreme left. *Author's collection*

Left: A view from the Walls c1925. Note the single span roof inserted in the centre of the original portion of the station. The roof over the Scarborough bays has gone but the fillets joining it to the original roof remain in place. The retaining wall on the extreme left supported one side of the roof covering the Scarborough platforms. The smoke is from the offices in the old hotel, each with its own coal fire. The 1906 offices are in the background. *Author's collection*

Below: The surviving portion of the Old Station roof and platforms in 1966, with the City Walls on the left. *Author's collection*

Above: **The 1839 arch through the City Walls, designed by G. T. Andrews and necessary to give access to the YNM/GNE station. In this 1964 view only one section remains of the original roof. A new office block spans the tracks and behind it are the top floor windows of the 1853 hotel, with two floors of the 1906 offices beyond. The micro-wave aerial for BR communications is mounted on the top of the 1906 building.** *R. F. Dean*

Selby and Leeds and in the first 32 days of operation 11,783½ passengers were carried and the receipts amounted to £1,435 6s 7d. The line was extended to Burton Salmon in May 1840, with road transport on to the North Midland station near Sheffield, and on 30 June the line was opened throughout from York to Altofts Junction, with the trains running through to Normanton and giving connections to London (Euston Square).

The new station at York was opened for Y&NM passenger traffic on 4 January 1841, but although the GNE was opened for goods traffic on the same day its passenger trains did not commence running until 30 March, due largely to delays in completing various structures on the line.

With the opening of the Great North of England a through route was available from London to Darlington, and in 1841 the Y&NM announced that it intended applying to Parliament for powers for a line from York to Scarborough, which had been under discussion for a couple of years. However, as the GNE was unable to proceed with its northern section between Darlington and Gateshead, George Hudson, with dreams of controlling much of the East Coast main line, stepped in to build the section north of Darlington, and to use existing links to reach Washington, Brockley Whins and Gateshead. This meant the postponement of the Scarborough branch until the

Darlington-Gateshead line was well under way, but in 1843 the York-Scarborough project was revived and approved at a special meeting held in November 1843.

The Darlington-Gateshead section was opened on 18 June 1844, completing the line from London to the Tyne and Hudson was already thinking of crossing the Tyne and continuing the length of Northumberland to the Tweed at Berwick — the last barrier before joining with the North British Railway to reach Edinburgh.

The York-Scarborough line was an easy one to construct and it was ready for opening on 7 July 1845, with a special train for Hudson and his guests: the public opening took place on the following day. At the same time a branch was opened from Rillington to Pickering to connect with the horse-drawn Whitby & Pickering Railway. Because of the light construction of the

Left: Later in 1966 a start was made on clearing the surviving remains of the Old Station. The original arch through the Walls is in the distance, and through the arch can be seen a section of Queen Street bridge.
R. F. Dean

Below: Hudson House, built on the site of the Old Station yard, was formally opened on 7 November 1968. It houses part of the staff of the Eastern Region headquarters, the Region formed when the Eastern and North Eastern Regions amalgamated from 1 January 1967. The photograph was taken from the City Walls. *BR*

Left: The roadway and footway arches through the City Walls adjacent to the North Postern. These were built to allow access into the City from the Great North of England Railway's coal depots on the river bank outside the Walls. The second arch is through the approach embankment to Lendal Bridge — one of the main road crossings over the River Ouse. *Author*

W&P through running was not possible, but over the next two years the Whitby & Pickering was improved and made fit for steam locomotives, so that in 1847 trains commenced to run through from the junction at Rillington to Whitby. At this stage, however, it was impossible to abolish the rope worked incline down from Goathland to Beck Hole, but in 1865 the North Eastern built a new line to the east of the old, over which locomotives could work and this remained in use until 1965: it has since been reopened by the North York Moors Railway — over which trains now operate between Pickering and Grosmont.

The next link in Yorkshire's growing chain of railways was the branch from York to Market Weighton, opened in October 1847; it had been intended to build through to Beverley to give access to Hull over the line from Bridlington, but this project was cut short because of Hudson's fall from grace and the Market Weighton-Beverley section was not completed until 1865.

Next came the East & West Yorkshire Junction Railway from York to Knaresborough, which reached the outskirts of the town in October 1848 but which took another three years to reach the centre! By that date the company, which had undergone many changes in its short life, had been taken over by the York & North Midland Railway, and in conjunction with the Leeds Northern Railway it was possible to reach Starbeck station; this accommodated Harrogate passengers until the new central station was opened at Harrogate in 1862.

Thus within the space of 10 years all the routes radiating from York were open, although there were some later developments which modified the routes. When in 1848 the Great Northern Railway was pushing northwards Hudson saw his monopoly being threatened and he made a shrewd and tactical move by building the three mile link between Burton Salmon and Knottingley, on the Wakefield, Pontefract & Goole line of the newly formed Lancashire & Yorkshire Railway. At the time the L&Y was completing a branch from Knottingley to join the Great Northern at Askern, $4\frac{1}{4}$ miles north of Doncaster, and Hudson's link easily and quickly provided a route from York to Doncaster, although it was delayed by the construction of the Aire bridge at Brotherton.

Seeing an easy eay of reaching York without the expense of building some 25 miles of line the Great Northern decided to forego its ambitions and settle for running powers over the L&Y and Y&NM into York, where it paid a rental for use of

Above: **A well-known view of the carriage sidings at the Old Station in the 1860s. These were originally the York & North Midland's coal depot sidings. Lendal Bridge in the distance.** *Author's collection*

the station. The Knottingley-Doncaster link was completed in August 1848 and for a couple of years the Burton Salmon-Knottingley gap was filled by a horse-bus service. With the completion by the Great Northern of the Peterborough-London line it became possible to reach London in August 1850, at first using a temporary terminus at Maiden Lane until King's Cross was ready in October 1852. In the meantime the tubular bridge at Brotherton had been completed.

The East Coast Route gradually acquired the

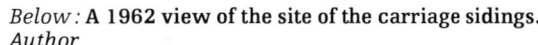

Below: **A 1962 view of the site of the carriage sidings.** *Author*

Left: In North Eastern days the yard at the Old Station was used to display new locomotives and rolling stock to the Directors when they were meeting in the Board Room in the 1906 offices. This 1922 view is of the pioneer Raven Pacific No 2400 (later named *City of Newcastle*) in 'shop grey', with electric express locomotive No 13 behind. *Author's collection*

Right: The 1841 station was built on a site once occupied by the Romans and during its construction a number of Roman baths were uncovered. Work in connection with the provision of an underground bunker to house the Control unearthed this skeleton. *BR*

Left: In later years many of the engines bound for Queen Street Museum were photographed in the Old Station yard before being placed on display. This is *Columbine*, dating from 1845 and the first engine built at Crewe Works for the Grand Junction Railway (which became part of the LNWR in the following year). The disproportionate cab, fitted to give increased protection to the crew, has now been removed and replaced by a more appropriate weatherboard. *LPC*

Right: With the building of the Scarborough branch (opened 1845) it was necessary to bridge the Ouse with this cast iron bridge. A public footpath was provided between the two tracks, with access by means of an internal stairway in each abutment, reached from the side arches. *Author's collection*

Left: The girders of Scarborough Bridge were renewed in 1874 in connection with the building of the new station, and the footpath was moved to the eastern side, with access by external stairways. When this view was taken in February 1950 the River Ouse was in flood — a hazard of life in the City — although the railway was not usually affected. Some trains bound for Scarborough were routed across the bridge on the up line and the semaphore signal controlled the crossover taking them on to their correct (down) line. *BR*

Right: Conversely some trains entering York station off the Scarborough line did so on the down line, as seen in this 1981 view of No 40.077. *W. K. Watson*

York-London trains, although it was another 50 years before the North Eastern ceased to use the description *main line* in the heading of the Normanton-York tables in the Working Timetable.

From 1840 York-Leeds trains used a roundabout route which had been devised by George Hudson to inflate the Y&NM's receipts. Instead of passing on to the Leeds & Selby Railway at Gascoigne Wood the trains continued to Castleford and then took the Whitwood Junction-Methley Junction curve to join the North Midland line into Leeds (Hunslet Lane), later extended to Wellington station in the centre of the city. Certainly the Leeds & Selby terminus at Marsh Lane was inconvenient, without connections to any other railway, and until 1869 the service between York and Leeds was provided by taking a York-Normanton train as far as Milford Junction, there changing into a Hull-Leeds (Wellington) train. This was a source of complaint, but in 1869 a new LNWR/NER joint station was opened in Leeds (adjacent to the Midland's Wellington station), reached from the east by extending the old Leeds & Selby route into the centre of the city. At the same time a new line was built from Church Fenton to Micklefield, giving a much shorter and quicker route to Leeds, although the old Leeds & Selby tunnel on the approach to Marsh Lane caused a bottleneck until it was opened out 25 years later. This allowed the NER to expand on the eastern side of Leeds, leading to the construction of Neville Hill engine shed and carriage sidings, and better facilities for Leeds-York (and Leeds-Hull) trains.

As East Coast traffic increased the route from York to Doncaster was becoming more and more inconvenient, relying as it did on the $10\frac{1}{2}$ mile stretch of Lancashire & Yorkshire metals between Knottingley and Askern Junction. Thus in 1863 the NER applied for powers to build two new lengths of line; these were from the old Y&NM route two miles south of York (later to be known as Chaloner Whin Junction) to Barlby, north of Selby, and from south of Selby to join the Great Northern at Owston (later to be known as Shaftholme Junction), only a few yards from the GN and L&Y end-on junction at Askern. Through Selby, over the River Ouse, the Hull and Selby line was to be used.

This new section of the East Coast main line was opened on 2 January 1871 and the Great Northern was given running powers to York. In exchange the North Eastern received running powers from Shaftholme Junction to Doncaster; this resulted in the Great Northern working main

Right: **A great drawback of the original station was that it was a terminus. In 1877 a fine new station was opened, with 13 platforms — all bays except two. It had to be built on a curve to fit in with the existing lines, but apart from extensions to the platforms it has undergone remarkably little change in its century of use. Platform signalbox was on the upper floor of the building to the right of the clock, and a footbridge later spanned the track at this spot, replacing the original subway.**
Crown Copyright, National Railway Museum, York

Below right: **For more than a century York has been a favourite centre for railway photographers. This fine view, taken about 1884, at the north end of the station, shows two spans of the roof, with in the background the station hotel as built. Note the contemporary NER standard signals with the lamps lower than the arms they served. The engine, built at Darlington in 1882, was withdrawn in 1907.** *LPC*

line expresses between Doncaster and York and the North Eastern the local service. However, for operating convenience, commencing in 1903, some expresses from King's Cross were taken over by North Eastern engines at Doncaster instead of York so that the York stop could be omitted.

When the Selby route was opened in 1871 East Coast trains were still using the original station at York, but from 1877 all passenger traffic was transferred to the new station, where the operating conditions were much better with the removal of the need to work through trains into a terminal station.

Since 1877 there has been little change in the lines radiating from York; the only branch actually entering York which has closed is that from Market Weighton, Beverley and Hull (in November 1965), although a York-Hull service is now provided via Selby, either by changing from York-Doncaster trains into Leeds-Hull trains, or by the three through trains which run via Church Fenton and Gascoigne Wood and enter Selby at the south end. Closures of more distant lines which affected York services were:

1 Bishophouse Junction (on the main line between Raskelf and Pilmoor) to Gilling, Coxwold and Pickering, which brought about the closure of the York-Pickering service on 2 February 1953.
2 Rillington-Pickering-Grosmont from 8 March 1965. This brought about the withdrawal of the York-Malton-Whitby service.

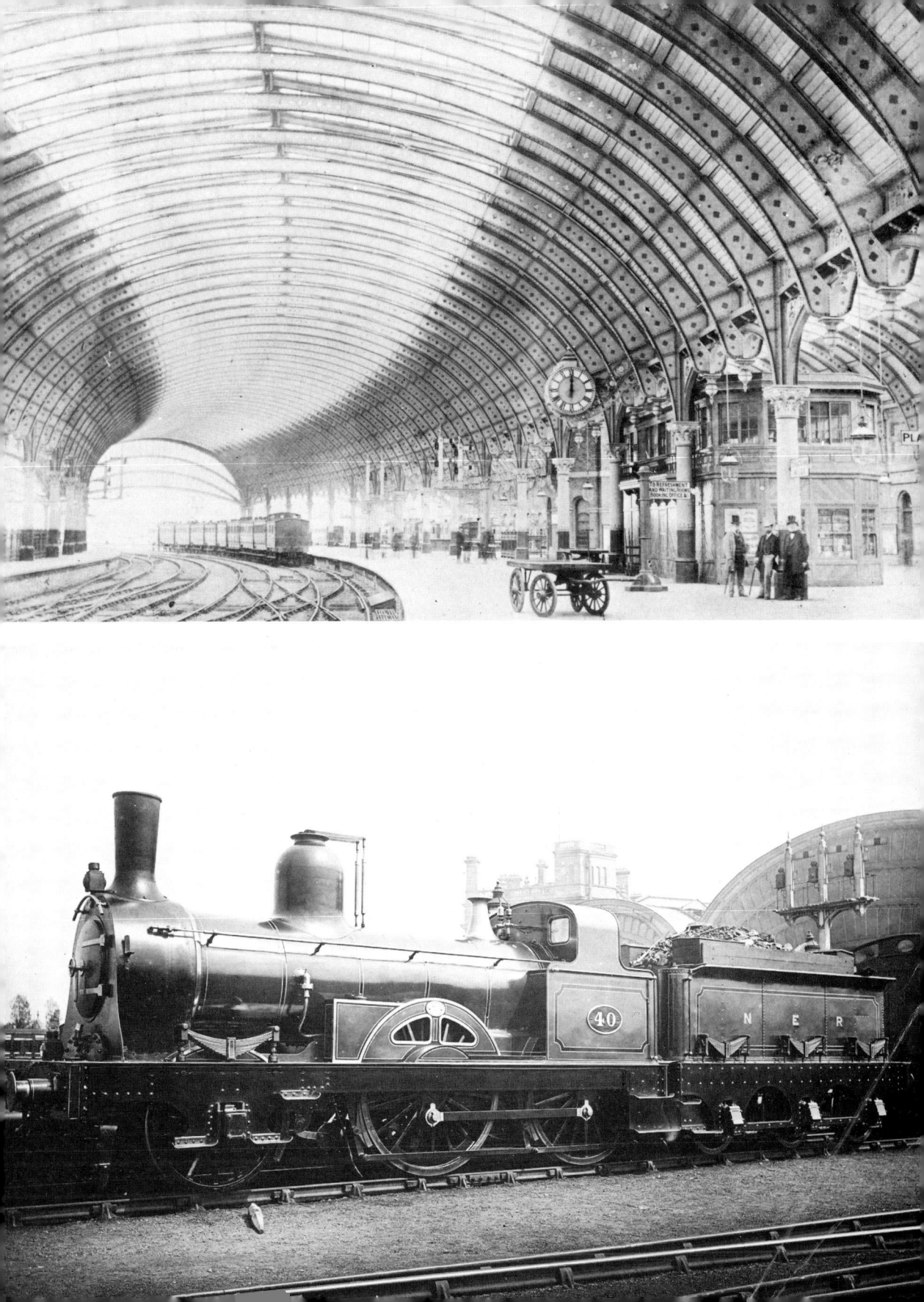

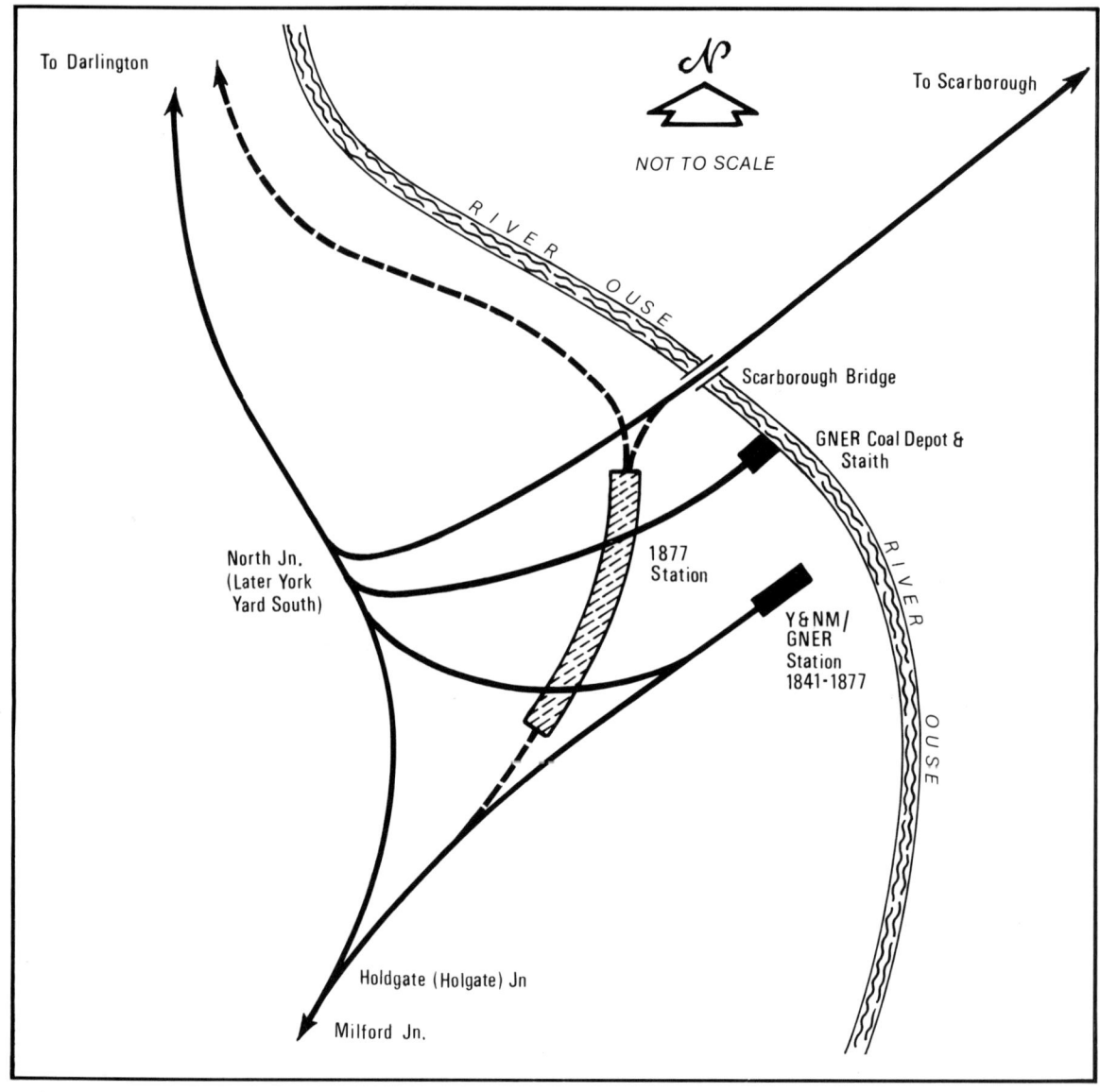

To Darlington

NOT TO SCALE

RIVER OUSE

Scarborough Bridge

To Scarborough

GNER Coal Depot & Staith

1877 Station

North Jn. (Later York Yard South)

Y & NM/ GNER Station 1841-1877

RIVER OUSE

Holdgate (Holgate) Jn

Milford Jn.

Above: **Arrangement of 1877 station to fit in with existing lines.**

The recent discovery of extremely valuable coal deposits in the area around Selby prompted the National Coal Board to develop a new coalfield just at the time British Rail was introducing High Speed Trains and drastically cutting journey times. The possibilities of pitfall slacks on a high speed line meant that to safeguard the route a strip of coal worth £1,080 million would have to remain untouched. An alternative route could easily have been made available by using the existing Selby Canal-Gascoigne Wood-Sherburn South-Church Fenton-York line, but this was not suitable for HSTs and an alternative scheme was considered and approved.

This involved building 14 miles of completely new high speed line to the west of Selby, from near Temple Hirst (on the existing main line) to join the four track Church Fenton-York line at Colton, five miles south-west of York. The cost would be £60 million — a small sum when compared with the value of the coal that would be released. British Rail has planned and supervised the new line on which work started on 4 April 1980, followed by the formal laying of the foundation stone on 30 July 1980. The contract for the construction of the trackbed and the building of various bridges was awarded to A. Monk & Co Ltd at £30 million.

The whole project is being paid for by the NCB and BR have gained a bonus in that Selby swing bridge over the River Ouse will no longer prove a hindrance to main line trains, although the bridge will have to remain in use for Hull-Selby-Leeds trains. The new route should be available for traffic in 1983 and high speed running will be introduced when the track has 'settled'. On completion it is planned to abandon the section of 1871 line between Barlby Junction (Selby) and Chaloners Whin Junction (York).

In September 1839 a start was made on clearing the site for the station at York; by that date the line towards Normanton had been partially opened and the arch through the City Walls had been completed, allowing wagons of coal to pass through to temporary sidings at Tanner's Moat. The first design for the station prepared by G. T. Andrews was ready in October 1839 but the cautious Darlington group controlling the Great

Above: **Seventy years later and steam still dominates the scene, again at the north end of the station. Colour light signals have replaced the semaphores and the hotel has been extended. The engine is the pioneer Gresley Pacific** *Great Northern* **as rebuilt by Edward Thompson.** *S. E. Teasdale*

Left: **Between 1899 and 1904 engines from five 'foreign' companies could be seen at York, in addition to the native North Eastern engines. The Midland reached York in 1879 via the Swinton & Kottingley Joint line, using 2-4-0 engines on the passenger trains. This is 59, later 196, for long a York engine.** *Author's collection*

North of England company considered it too ambitious, and it was only at the third attempt that agreement on the design was reached, in March 1840. In the following month the York & North Midland advertised for tenders for the building of the station, with a closing date of 7 May 1840, and when they were opened it was found that they ranged from £7,886.6s to £11,800 and the lowest, submitted by Holroyd & Waller of Sheffield, was accepted, with a completion date set at 30 August! The ironwork and glazing of the train shed roof was let separately to Bingley & Co of Leeds but it was soon reported that Mr Bingley was not proceeding satisfactorily, and difficulty was experienced along Tanner Row, where a retaining wall had to be built.

The station facing Tanner Row consisted of a two-storey block having passenger facilities and offices, with the booking hall in the centre; the ground floor was faced in sandstone and the upper floor was built of a matching yellow brick but with sandstone facings to the windows etc. The train-shed behind the offices had a platform down each side — the departure platform immediately behind the offices and the arrival platform on the opposite side — but the roof was not continuous across the tracks and a 16ft gap was left down the centre. Thus one side of each roof span was supported by the buildings, with the other side supported on cast iron columns. Both ends of the train shed were walled, with arches at the south end to allow the trains to enter, and a contemporary drawing, probably by

Andrews himself, shows large rectangular openings at the buffer-stop end, making for a very draughty station! The wall and arches at the south end were abolished as the platforms were extended. A section was later inserted in the roof to join the two spans, thus providing continuous cover between the buildings.

The upper floor of the office block housed the Board Room and the half-yearly meeting held on 29 January 1841 was the first to be held there, although it was not quite complete.

It was soon realised that goods facilities should be provided at the station and on 22 April 1841 a tender of £4,950 was accepted for a 'merchandise

Below: **The Great Eastern reached York in 1891, using the Great Northern from Doncaster to Shaftholme Junction and the North Eastern thence to York. For a time the GE trains were worked by these Holden singles and No 12, with extended smokebox, was photographed at York South shed.** *LPC*

Above right: **The Great Northern was the first 'foreign' company to reach York, running from Doncaster via Knottingley, Burton Salmon and Church Fenton. In the present century the heaviest East Coast expresses, which were worked by Great Northern engines south of York, were handled by the large Ivatt Atlantics, such as No 293, photographed at York South shed.** *L&GRP, courtesy David & Charles*

Right: **The Great Central also stationed an Atlantic at York for working its trains and this is No 262 at South Points.** *Author's collection*

station', again with designs by Andrews and this building remained in use until BR days, latterly known as the 'Sack Warehouse'. The Y&NM coal and lime depot was at first inside the Walls, on sidings which ran towards the river.

The Great North of England coal depot was outside the Walls and included a staith on the river bank where Durham coal could be tipped into vessels on the Ouse. To get the coal into the city by road required a roundabout journey via Thief Lane, Queen Street and Micklegate, crossing the tracks into the station and passing through the Walls at Micklegate Bar. To simplify matters the GNE persuaded the Corporation (with payment of a premium of £55) to allow an arch to be cut through the Walls adjacent to North Street Postern to give direct access to the North Street area of the City. The arch, again to the designs of G. T. Andrews, was built in 1840 by John Buckley with a successful tender of £380. The arch, flanked by two footway arches, still exists, although the inscribed boundary stone built into the north facing wall, below the parapet, has disappeared. When Lendal Bridge (road) was finally opened in 1863 the southern approach embankment spanned the road through the arch.

The coal depot tracks sloped down towards the river and in August 1871 a train of 20 wagons loaded with coal ran down the slope and plunged into the river one after the other! The coal and lime depots on the river bank remained in use until the 1870s, when they were closed with the building of the new station and hotel.

The 1841 station was soon found to be too small, with very restricted access through the Walls, and in 1846 a second arch was built, identical with the first. Later the same year a start was made in forming two new platforms outside the original station, between the refreshment room block on the arrival platform and the Walls. This meant cutting back the earth ramparts and building a retaining wall high enough to support one side of the roof of the new train-shed; the other side of the roof was carried on cast iron columns and the section between the old and new roofs was also roofed over. The two new platforms were known as the Scarborough bays as they were built to handle the additional traffic generated by the opening of the Scarborough branch in July 1845, but soon the station also had to accommodate the Market Weighton trains (October 1847), the Knaresborough trains (October 1848) and trains from Doncaster and the south (1850).

On 22 February 1853 a station hotel was opened, built in a cramped position at the terminal ends of the platforms, to a design by Andrews; since the downfall of Hudson very little railway work had been commissioned from Andrews and he died in 1855. The hotel stood across the end of the office block on the departure platform, and the refreshment room block on the arrival platform, and both these were soon extended to form an interlocking block of buildings. Eventually, when the hotel became redundant on the opening in 1878 of the hotel at the new station, access was made from the former hotel into the two wings and since then the whole of the accommodation has been used as offices.

When it became redundant the old station train shed was used for storing coaches, but in the 1960s all the tracks in the station and yard were cleared to make way for the new Hudson House office block needed to house the combined North Eastern and Eastern Region staffs, which became known as the Eastern Region from 1 January 1967.

The demolition included the Sack Warehouse — formerly the Merchandise station — and the remaining portions of the train-shed, although a small section across the ends of the platforms, adjacent to the former hotel, was allowed to remain to cover the space allocated for the storage of bicycles used by the staff! The train-shed covering the Scarborough bays had vanished many

years earlier, at a date not yet located, but photographs of NER steam road wagons taken in 1905 show a small portion of the roof in the background, with the spandrels identical with those used at Scarborough in 1845. At the north end a brick building had been erected inside the train-shed and this housed the horse-drawn steam fire engine allocated to York No 1 Brigade manned by NER staff. Similar volunteer brigades were based at the Wagon Works (No 2 Brigade) and the Carriage Works (No 3 Brigade). In the 1950s these platforms were occasionally used for exhibitions of rolling stock, such as the Festival of Britain display in 1951, and the Royal Coaches in 1958. From the summer of 1956 one platform was used as an end-loading dock for the Car Sleeper service.

During the course of their official travels, officials of the North Eastern Railway noticed many old pieces of railway equipment and these were collected together at York and eventually formed the nucleus of the LNER Railway Museum. This was in two sections, with the engines and larger items on display in the former Y&NM Works at Queen Street, and the smaller items, together with the documents and photographs, in what had originally been the First Class Refreshment Room at the Old Station. This was brought into use in 1928 and at various times there were suggestions that the train-shed of the Old Station should be used for the Queen Street items but this was found to be impractical.

Both sections of the museum closed because of World War 2 but reopened after the war and the Small Exhibits section remained in use until 17 December 1966, when increased space provided at Queen Street allowed the items to be moved there. Now, of course, the items are under the control of the National Railway Museum.

Hudson House was built on the site of the Old Station Yard and opened on 7 November 1968 by the then Chairman of the British Railways Board, Sir Henry Johnson. The design, approved by the Royal Fine Arts Commission, comprises four blocks of offices, two of four storeys and two of six storeys, linked together to form an internal court, with the staircases and lifts projecting from the links. The total floor area amounts to approximately 134,000sq ft. The grouping of the blocks is arranged with the taller blocks against Toft Green and the four-storey blocks nearest the City Walls so that the latter are not dominated by the buildings. The complex honours the name of George Hudson, the one-time York draper, who gained a taste for railways and all that entailed. He is also

Right: The Lancashire & Yorkshire Railway worked a number of trains into York, usually using 4-4-0, 4-4-2 or 4-6-0 engines, and this is No 1402 (later LMS No 10310) awaiting a westbound working. Note the amount of coal piled up in the tender, and the door from the cab on to the running plate. *W. L. Good*

Left: **The North Eastern Atlantics ruled the York-Edinburgh section of the main line for 20 years, and then put in another 20 years on secondary duties. No 532 was the first to be built and was photographed at York awaiting a return working to Newcastle.** *LPC*

Right: **As befitted its importance York provided extensive accommodation for the engines based there, and for those visiting the city, with running sheds both north and south of the station. The North shed was built to serve the 1877 station and housed the larger North Eastern engines. At first the building consisted of three roundhouses under one roof, with a fourth added in 1915.**
Author's collection

Above: Diesel traction on East Coast expresses was introduced in June 1958, and in January 1959 the prototype 'Deltic' locomotive arrived at York for trials. It is seen here leaving for the south. *C. Ord*

Left: In 1977 High Speed Trains made their appearance on regular workings and in May 1978 they began working on accelerated schedules, covering the 188 miles to London in 128 minutes. The pioneer production set for the East Coast is leaving York for the north in September 1977. *BR*

Below left: The opening of the National Railway Museum in September 1975 has made York an important steam centre, not only because of the use of engines from the national collection, but also as a base for visiting engines. One of the first tasks of the Museum — even before it was formally opened by the Duke of Edinburgh — was to provide engines for display at the exhibition and Cavalcade held at Shildon in August 1975, and here are two GN engines (*Henry Oakley* hauling Stirling No 1) leaving York for Shildon. *E. Sanderson*

remembered by nearby George Hudson Street, renamed from Railway Street in 1971, and his house at 44 Monkgate is marked by a plaque. Indirectly Hudson's memory is also marked by the numerous buildings he commissioned from his architect, George Townsend Andrews, but Hudson is best remembered for the railway system he shaped, which still lives on in the ancient City of York.

Now High Speed Trains and locomotive-hauled Inter City trains pass through the station so frequently as to be commonplace, carrying passengers between London, the south-west, the northeast, and Scotland. They are carried in a fraction of the time and in a standard of comfort that Hudson could never have envisaged, although his plans for lines between London and Edinburgh did reach fruition in his lifetime; however it was not until 1923 that the East Coast Route came under the control of one company. The goods traffic, which reached its peak in small four-wheel

unbraked wagons, is now moved — what there is left of it — in fully braked trains, with the guard riding on the engine, harking back to the early days of railways where, on some lines, the guard rode in a shelter on the tender, looking back along the train to see that all was present and correct. Such is progress!

Below: **An aerial view of York giving an excellent view of the railway layout. The key to the locations is: 1 1877 station, south end; 2 Queen Street; 3 Erecting shops, Loco works; 4 Y&NM locomotive works; 5 Holgate Villa offices; 6 Holgate (Bridge) Junction; 7 South shed; 8 Public footbridge; 9 Carriage works; 10 Wagon works; 11 Footbridge joining carriage and wagon works; 12 Down yard; 13 Up yard; 14 York Yard North; 15 Skelton sidings; 16 River Ouse; 17 Clifton carriage sidings; 18 District Engineer's yard; 19 Locomotive coaling plant; 20 Goods warehouse, Leeman Road; 21 Branches yard.**
K. C. Appleby collection

Development of Passenger Services

From 1 July 1840, when it was first possible to travel from York to London by train, the service was advertised with departures from York at 7.30am, 9.00am, 12.30pm and 4.00pm, arriving at London (Euston Square) at 6.45pm, 7.00pm, 11.30pm and 5.30am respectively. The North Midland notice announcing the new service stated 'Passengers arriving in Derby by any of the above trains can proceed on, without change of carriage, either to Leeds or Birmingham, after remaining at Derby for half-an-hour for Refreshment'. In the down direction the 6.00am, 9.30am and 8.30pm from London arrived in York at 4.30pm, 7.15pm and 9.45am. Some alterations took place from 30 October 1840, but the weekday times when the permanent station opened on 4 January 1841 were:

For Leeds, Selby and Hull: 8.00am, 10.45am, 3.15pm and 5.45pm.
From Leeds for York, Selby and Hull: 8.00am, 10.45am, 3.15pm and 5.45pm.
From York to London, Birmingham, Derby, Sheffield and Wakefield: 6.30am, 8.45am, 11.00am, 4.00pm and 6.00pm (Mail).
Fares announced at the same time were:

From York to:	1st Class	2nd Class	3rd Class
London	£2-16s-0d	£1-17s-6d	—*
Birmingham	£1-12s-0d	£1-1s-6d	—*
Derby	£1-2s-0d	14s-6d	—
Sheffield	13s-6d	9s-0d	—
Leeds	6s-0d	4s-6d	3s-0d
Manchester	£1-0s-0d	13s-0d	9s-6d
Selby	3s-6d	2s-6d	2s-0d
Hull	8s-6d	6s-0d	4s-6d

*By 'Mail' 1st class £2-18s-6d; 2nd Class £2-1s-0d

For the first six months of operation using the permanent station the receipts were quoted as £31,656-10s-6d and the expenses as £12,014-12s-6d.
The Great North of England notice for the opening of the line between York and Darlington on 31 March 1841 quoted the fare as 12/- 1st class and 9/- 2nd class, and also gave the rates for horses and carriages, with 'Parties riding in their own Carriages, and childrenj under 7 years of age, at lower rates'. Trains left York at 6.00am, 7.20am (Mail), 9.35am, 2.30pm and 6.00pm, arriving at Darlington at 8.30am, 9.25am, 12.05pm, 5.00pm and 8.30pm respectively, all except the Mail taking $2\frac{1}{2}$hr for the 44 miles.

In June 1844 the service was extended to Gateshead, and with the opening of the temporary bridges across the Tyne and Tweed in 1848, to Edinburgh and Glasgow.

In 1840 the 9.30am from London was due in York at 7.15pm, $9\frac{3}{4}$hr, but by 1847 the time was down to 6hr 10min, and this was gradually reduced with the opening of the Great Northern route to London (Maiden Lane) on 7 August 1850,

Above right: **In the decade 1873 to 1883 the East Coast expresses north of York were worked by the famous Fletcher '901' class of 2-4-0, with the trains made up of East Coast Joint Stock 6-wheel coaches. No 910 is standing at the north end of York station in the 1880s, probably awaiting passengers who are hurriedly eating their lunch during the meal stop! The engine was on display at the Stockton & Darlington 50th, 100th and 150th anniversary celebrations in 1875, 1925 and 1975 respectively, and it now forms part of the national collection housed at York. It was actually stationed at York shed when withdrawn from service in January 1925.** *LPC*

Right: **At the north end of the station the four bay platforms were used by trains from Scarborough and Hull; they could not be used by main line trains. This c1885 view shows the pioneer Stockton & Darlington 4-4-0 No 1160 (originally 160 *Brougham*), one of the two engines built with large double side window cabs for working over the exposed Stainmore route between Barnard Castle and Kirkby Stephen. The engine, built in 1860 and scrapped in 1888, is standing at the head of a train in what is now Platform 4, with the trees in the background in the garden of the hotel.** *LPC*

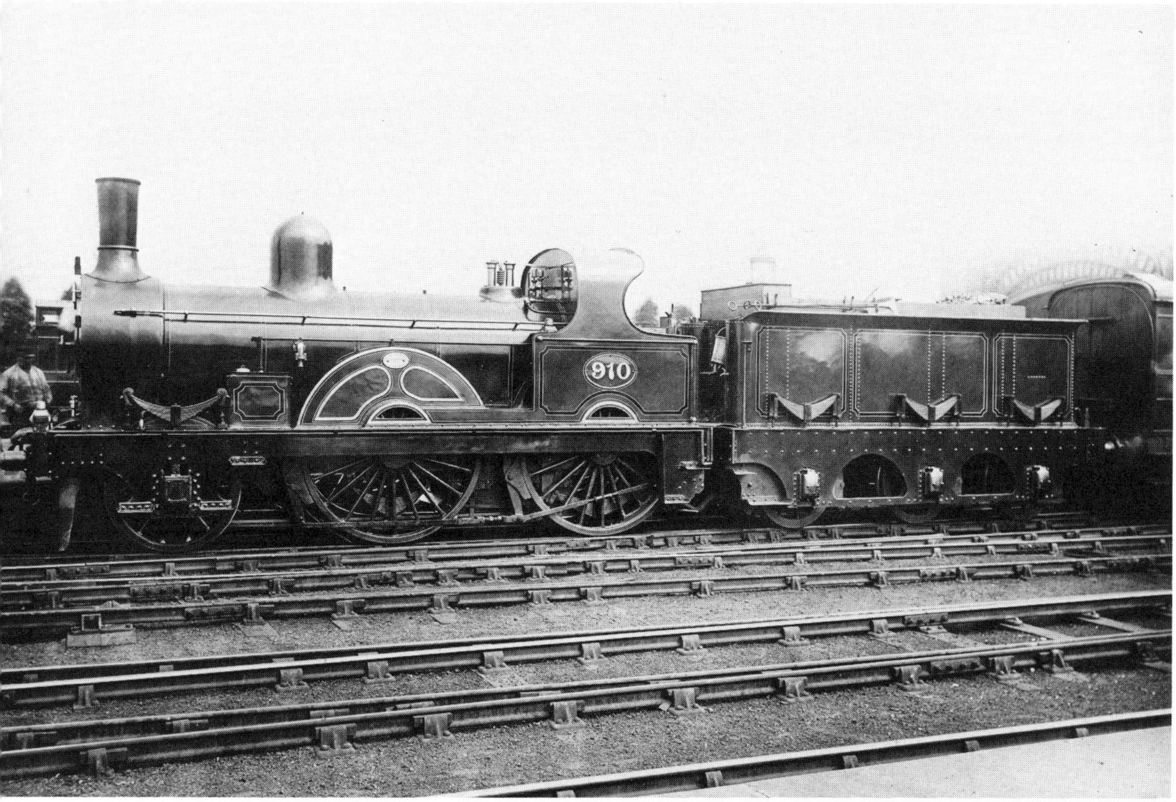
910

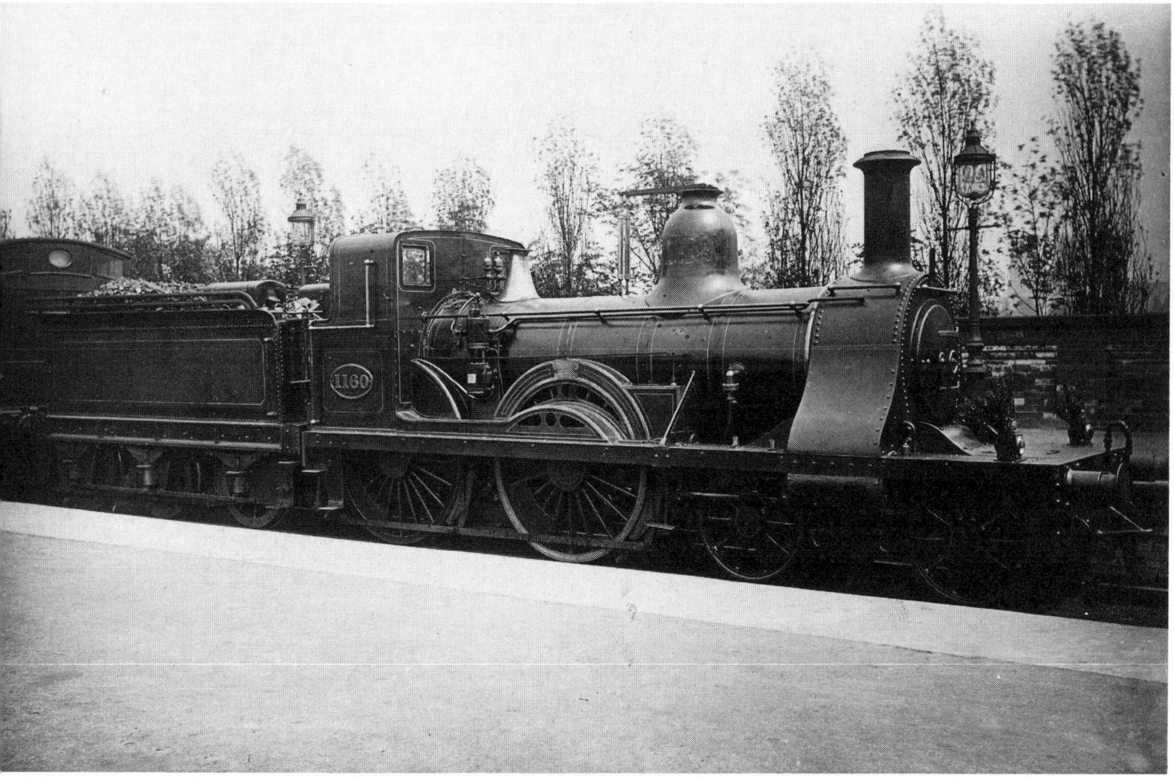
1160

the opening of the Retford-Peterborough direct line on 1 August 1852, and King's Cross station on 14 October 1852, so that by the final year of the Knottingley route (1870) the 10.00am from King's Cross was into York at 2.40pm, going forward at 3.00pm to arrive at Edinburgh at 8.30pm.

Using the new Selby route from 1871 brought the time down to 4hr 10min to York and 9½hr to Edinburgh, with a 30min lunch stop at York, and the timetables for the period included 'Passengers by the through trains between London and Scotland are conveyed in through carriages of the most improved description, the joint property of the Companies forming the East Coast Route, and especially constructed for the accommodation of this traffic'. By this date East Coast Joint Stock vehicles had been in use for 10 years and the arrangement was to continue for another 50 — in fact until the formation of the LNER. However, during this period there was little acceleration in Anglo-Scottish services and even in the 1930s the 10.00am from King's Cross took only 27min less to York in its winter timings, calling at 1.43pm to 1.49pm and reaching Edinburgh at the regular time of 6.15pm.

The start of general accelerations in 1932 brought the 10.00am into York at 1.33pm, with an arrival in Edinburgh at 5.50pm but, of course, in the summer months from 1928 the 'Flying Scotsman' had not called at York, and the fastest train was the down 'Scarborough Flier', which left King's Cross at 11.10am and was into York at 2.10pm. The 'Coronation' streamlined express, introduced on 5 July 1937, reduced the time still further, to 2hr 37min and this was not improved upon until the introduction of diesel traction. Now the High Speed Train service has brought the London-York time down to below 2hr! Even York to Darlington now takes only 28min by many trains — and it is not so long ago that 43min for the 44.1 miles was considered good going.

High Speed Trains first appeared at York in

Below: In 1885 the 'Tennant' 2-4-0 engines were the latest in a long line of North Eastern 2-4-0s but in this view, taken 40 years later, the pioneer engine, No 1463, has been relegated to working slow passenger trains between Darlington and York. It was photographed at Poppleton Junction, with the Harrogate branch diverging to the left. *H. L. Salmon*

Above right: At the southern extremity of the York area Class V Atlantic No 697 is approaching Chaloner Whin Junction on the 10am from Edinburgh, when the NER engine worked through from Newcastle to Doncaster. *R. J. Purves*

Right: The largest North Eastern engines used on the East Coast route were the short-lived Raven Pacifics. This location, north of the station, was a favourite viewpoint for photographers, although shots could be affected by smoke blowing across from engines standing in the shed yard on the right. The engine on this heavy down express is No 2401, named *City of Kingston upon Hull* by the LNER but still carrying its large brass North Eastern numberplates. As an indication of the indecision regarding a new livery the tender carries no lettering whatsoever. *Real Photographs*

June 1973 when on trial, but it was another four years before the first production unit for the East Coast, No 254.001, was formally handed over to the Eastern Region General Manager. This took place at a ceremony held on 7 September 1977, when five trumpeters from the Royal Scots Dragoon Guards (standing on the footbridge above Platform 9) played a specially written fanfare entitled '001'. At first the HSTs were run on locomotive timings, but from 8 May 1978 accelera-tions brought the London-York time down to 128min. This was reduced to 118min from 17 May 1982.

In the 1840s branches were opened from York to Scarborough, Market Weighton and Knares-borough. The line to Scarborough played a large part in the development of the resort as a fashion-able seaside holiday centre, restricted at first to visitors able to spend many weeks in the town, but later the popularity of the day excursion saw

Left: From 1924 the Gresley Pacifics were the mainstay of the main line over the whole distance between London and Edinburgh. For a time it was the practice to change engines at York, where on southbound trains the North Eastern Area engine handed over to a Southern Area engine. Here No 2559 *The Tetrarch* is pulling out of the station heading south, photographed from the footbridge and signal gantry adjoining Locomotive Yard signalbox. A '3P' 4-4-0 (No 774?) is standing outside Queen Street shed. *Real Photographs*

Centre left: Favourites on the East Coast route were the Gresley 'A4' Pacifics, first built in 1935 for working the 'Silver Jubilee' streamlined express between London and Newcastle, although subsequently used on both streamlined and non-streamlined trains. This is No 60028 *Walter K. Whigham* at a late stage in its life, leaving York for King's Cross in 1961 after the Queen and the Duke of Edinburgh had attended the wedding of the Duke of Kent in York Minster. The second and third vehicles are the East Coast Royal saloons. *E. Sanderson*

Bottom left: The final Pacifics for the East Coast route were the Peppercorn engines, with No 60154, formerly *Bon Accord*, on the 08.45 Leeds-Glasgow train on 10 July 1965. The engine is crossing the up and down Scarborough Goods lines and also visible are the connections into Platforms 14 and 15 from the Scarborough direction. This section of the layout has now been modified and the Scarborough connections abolished, so that the northern end of Platform 14 (in the foreground) could be widened and curved to suit the main line. Previously northbound trains had to stop south of the footbridge. *Ian S. Carr*

train after train leaving York for the coast. At first the regular trains ran only between York and Scarborough, but eventually blossomed into through services to and from such places as London, Southampton, Bournemouth, Liverpool and Glasgow; however, most of these trains ran only during the summer months when the demand was largest, and during the winter months the service was provided by Leeds-York-Scarborough trains. For the last 25 years the regular services on this route have been provided by multiple-unit railcars, but 1982 has seen the introduction of a locomotive hauled Scarborough-York-Liverpool service.

The York-Market Weighton service was extended to Hull in 1865 with the opening of the section on to Beverley, but for much of its life this branch warranted only a purely local service, with most trains stopping at all the stations. However, the introduction of trains stopping only at the market-town stations at Beverley, Market Weighton and Pocklington, gave a better service from Hull to the north, with connections at York. It was over this branch that York saw its first DMU services when Hull units commenced working in on certain trains from 29 July 1957. The branch was closed in November 1965.

At first the Knaresborough branch service amounted to only three trains a day, stopping at all stations, but with the opening of a new central station at Harrogate in 1862 the service began to improve and there was soon an express in both directions, stopping only at Knaresborough. One notable working was the morning Bradford-York train, worked by a North Eastern engine out-stationed at the Midland shed at Manningham, and in 1937 the 'Yorkshire Pullman' commenced running via York but in the up direction only.

Apart from being reduced to single line in places this branch has changed little and a York-Harrogate service still operates.

Perhaps the greatest change affecting York was the opening of the Swinton & Knottingley Joint line in 1879 and first to take advantage of this was the Midland Railway, which built up a network of services based on its York-Sheffield trains, most running through to London (St Pancras) or Bristol. Twenty years later the Great Central developed similar services reaching as far as the south coast. These services were of advantage to the North Eastern in that all the passengers from the south, except those for York itself, had to be carried forward by the North Eastern, which had the monopoly of the services to all the towns on the north-east coast from Hull to Berwick.

On the Scarborough branch at the turn of the century some trains were booked to cover the 42 miles in 55min, with a 3min stop at Malton, but even by 1980, using DMU, this had only become 52min but with two stops, at Malton and Seamer. With the introduction of the full Liverpool-Scarborough service from 17 May 1982 the York-Scarborough booking is now 49min, still with two

Below: **An important secondary service has for many years been provided by the Scarborough-York-Leeds trains and, in fact, many of these have now been extended to Liverpool using locomotive hauled stock. For 60 years or so the trains were worked by 4-4-0 engines ranging from the North Eastern Class F of 1886 to the LNER 'D49' of 1934, but in the 1920s the Class Q (LNER D17/2) were commonplace, including 1908, seen hauling a mixed train of NER clerestory, elliptical and straight-sided stock.**
T. G. Hepburn/Rail Archive Stephenson

stops. The train which caused most interest was the summer 4.45pm from Bradford, which ran non-stop from Leeds to Scarborough, 67¾ miles, in 75min; it was due through York at 5.41pm in 28min from Leeds, leaving 47min for the 42mile journcy to Scarborough. This cxprcss was introduced in 1900 for Leeds and Bradford businessmen who had rented a house in Scarborough for their family for two or three months, and it enabled them to travel to their office in the West Riding after an early breakfast and return to the coast in time for their evening meal.

For many years Scarborough was well served by trains to and from King's Cross, particularly in the summer months, culminating in the 'Scarborough Flier' introduced by the LNER. For engine changing purposes this train always stopped at York, with a booking of 50min from York to Scarborough without a stop. On Saturdays, when there were sufficient passengers for Scarborough, without the need to serve York, the train was re-engined on the down main line, denying access to or from the platform.

Re-introduced in June 1950 the 'Scarborough Flyer' — note slight change in spelling — ran at weekends only in the summer, but poor facilities and the change in holiday habits led to its demise.

The fastest time on the branch from York to Hull was accomplished by the diesel-electric railcar which operated intermittently in the 1930s: unfortunately the Hull car, *Lady Hamilton*, was not reliable and often a steam hauled train had to be put on at short notice when

Above left: **Scarborough was a popular seaside resort, both for day trippers and longer stay holidaymakers. Many trains from Lancashire and the Midlands were made up of LMS stock and hauled to York by LMS engines. Favourite engines to haul these 13-coach trains from York to Scarborough and back were the 'B16' 4-6-0s chosen from York's large fleet of these engines, and this is No 2368 leaving the down main line and taking the Scarborough line at the north end of the station.** *Real Photographs*

Left: **A handbill for an evening excursion to Scarborough offering 84 miles of travel for 2s 1d! The present Day Return fare is £3.80.** *Author's collection*

Above: **Scarborough-Leeds trains were often re-engined at York, with an engine off a Newcastle-King's Cross train taking over for the journey to Leeds. Leaving York on such a working, and running on the Up Leeds line, is the Gresley water-tube boiler engine No 10000 in the early 1930s.** *C. Ord*

the railcar was unavailable. The car, at 4.48pm from York, was allowed 52min non-stop over the 42 miles, whereas the steam worked Newcastle-Hull dining car express at 2.35pm from York was allowed one minute longer with a stop at Beverley.

The local services to Haxby, Strensall and Flaxton on the Scarborough line, and to Earswick on the Hull line, were worked in the 1920s by 'BTP' 0-4-4T on 'autocars' and various types of petrol engined railcars, including the Leyland road bus with rail wheels.

The fastest trains on the Harrogate branch in the 1930s were the 8.25am from Harrogate (30min with two stops) and the 5.15pm from York (with one stop). On Sundays in summer the service was worked by Sentinel steam railcars stopping only at Starbeck and Knaresborough. The up 'Yorkshire Pullman' when re-routed via York in 1937 was allowed 25min for the $20\frac{1}{2}$ miles.

Great Northern

A route from York to Doncaster via Burton Salmon and Knottingley became available in April 1850 with the opening of a temporary bridge across the River Aire at Brotherton, and although at first used only for goods traffic its use for passenger traffic was authorised three months later. On 7 August 1850 the Great Northern commenced services through from Doncaster to London, using at first a temporary station at Maiden Lane pending completion of the permanent station at King's Cross. Connecting services were provided to York by the 6.00am, 7.40am, 10.30am and 6.00pm departures from Maiden Lane, and trains from York arrived in London at 7.30am, 6.45pm, 8.40pm and 9.00pm.

On 25 November 1848 the York & North Midland had reached a formal agreement with the Great Northern regarding through traffic between York and Doncaster, allowing the GN to station four engines at York, and the Y&NM two engines at Doncaster, and this was ratified by a

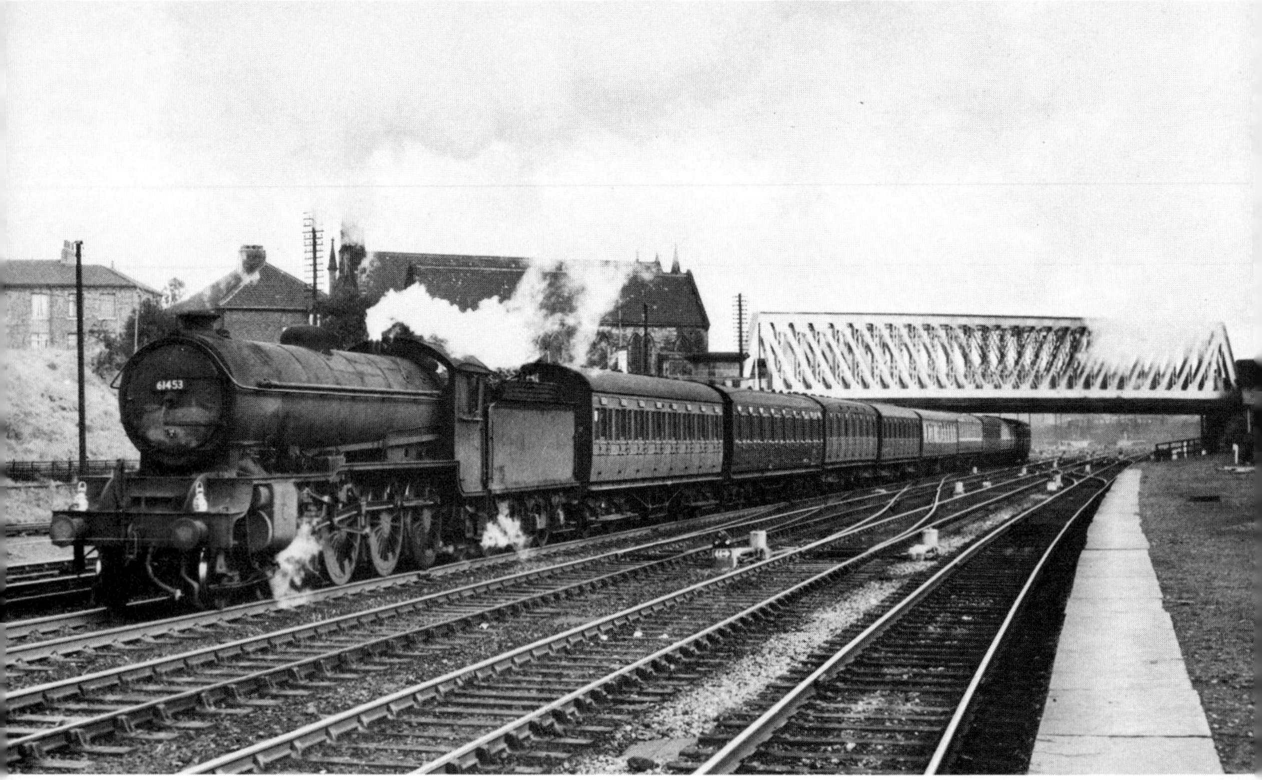
61453

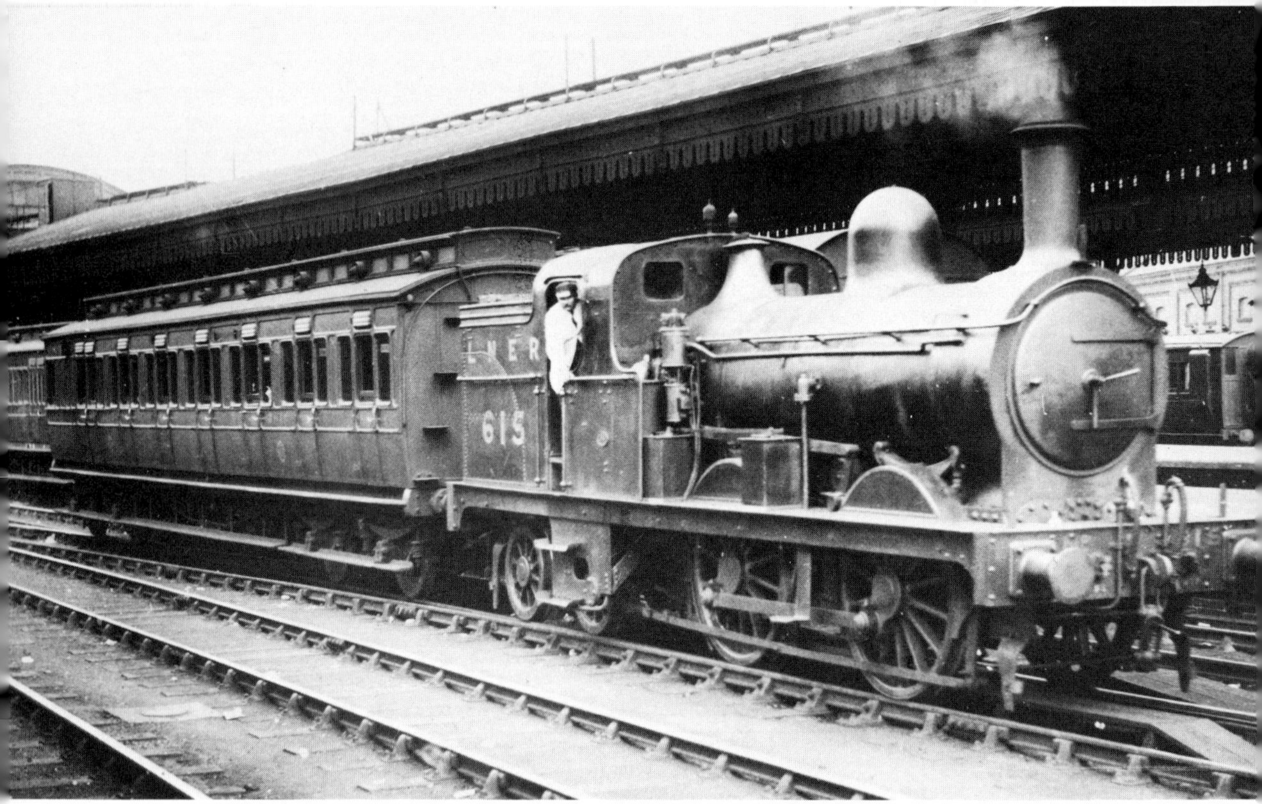
L N E R
615

Left: In British Railways' days the 'B16' 4-6-0s were still being used on passenger trains, such as No 61453 — one of the engines rebuilt to 'B16/3' — passing Holgate Platforms in 1956, again on the Up Leeds line. *Author*

Below left: **York had a small network of local services with 'BTP' 0-4-4T engines on one-coach or two-coach push-and-pull units running to Strensall on the Scarborough branch, Earswick on the Hull branch, and Copmanthorpe on the Leeds line. A similar unit worked in from Selby each day after running a trip on the Cawood branch and this is No 615 leaving York for Selby in August 1926.** *Author's collection*

Top right: **In July 1922 the NER introduced a Leyland bus with rail wheels and this was used on the local services. To save turning the bus it was adapted to be driven from either end, and here it is leaving York for Strensall, being driven from a small driving compartment at the far end. It is running in the down direction on the Up line, with the semaphore signal in the 'off' position to take it over the crossover on to the down line, no other route being permissible.** *Author's collection*

Centre right: **Excursions were often worked by 'J21' 0-6-0 engines, the fact that this is an excursion being indicated by the rake of six-wheel coaches between two bogie brake thirds — an elliptical roofed vehicle at the front and a clerestory roofed coach at the rear. The train, running with Express Passenger headlamps, is leaving York heading north.** *H. L. Salmon*

Bottom right: **Three diesel-electric railcars were purchased from Armstrong-Whitworth and stationed at Middlesbrough, Leeds and Hull. The Leeds car, *Northumbrian*, was used on a circular Leeds-York-Harrogate-Leeds service, seen here leaving York for Harrogate in 1935 hauling a North Eastern clerestory coach to provide additional accommodation.** *Real Photographs*

supplementary agreement dated 25 November 1850. These arrangements continued in force when the North Eastern Railway was formed four years later, but with the opening of the NER line from Chandlers Whin Junction (2 miles south of York) to Shaftholme Junction ($4\frac{1}{4}$ miles north of Doncaster) in 1871 the use of the Knottingley route decreased, although a local Doncaster-Knottingley-York service continued until 1912. Even then passenger trains continued to use the Doncaster-Knottingley-Church Fenton line for a London-Harrogate service until 1949. An unusual use of the Knottingley route was made in the 1930s when the 11.25am Lincoln-York (12.20pm from Doncaster) left the main line at Shaftholme Junction and ran via the old main line to allow a clear run for the King's Cross-Edinburgh non-stop due to pass Doncaster at 12.40pm and York at 1.10pm. The Lincoln train arrived at York at 1.12pm.

Another GN service to York was provided by using the Wakefield (West Riding & Grimsby) line

Above: British Railways introduced diesel railcars in 1954 and they were first used between Bradford-Leeds (Central) and Harrogate, soon spreading throughout the Region. Within 15 years steam traction had ceased and dieselisation was complete, and this became the typical scene, with Nos 45.053, 55.021 *Argyll & Sutherland Highlander* and a DMU. The railcar is in Platform 15 and No 45.053 in Platform 14. *W. K. Watson*

Top: 'Deltic' No 55.008 *The Green Howards* leaving Platform 14 for the north. Note the simplified layout with no connections to the Scarborough branch; the widened north end of the platform can also be seen. Also visible is the building housing the electric signalbox and relay room etc, built on Platform 14 and brought into use in 1951. *N. E. Stead*

Above: For a time steam and diesel locomotives were used side by side, although in this view No D5655 is piloting a 'B1' 4-6-0 passing Holgate Platforms. *C. Ord*

Top left: **The production series of 22 'Deltic' locomotives revitalised the passenger services on the East Coast route, with speeds unheard of in steam days. No D9003** *The King's Own Yorkshire Light Infantry* **leaves for the north with the down 'Flying Scotsman'.** *C. Ord*

Centre left: **The greatest feature of the 'Deltics' once they had settled down, was their availability and it was possible to see some locomotives through York three times in 24 hours as they raced backwards and forwards between London and Edinburgh. This is No D9009** *Alycidon* **on the up 'Flying Scotsman' passing Holgate platforms.** *C. Ord*

Bottom left: **Prototype HST No 252 001 arriving at York in 1974. The floodlighting towers illuminate the north end shunting neck of Dringhouses Up Yard.** *E. Sanderson*

Above: **Victor and vanquished! HST No 254 001 standing in Platform 8A, with No 55.017** *The Durham Light Infantry* **passing on the down 'Flying Scotsman' in September 1977.** *E. Sanderson*

out of Doncaster as far as South Elmsall, there taking the Swinton & Knottingley Joint curve to join the S&K line to Ferrybridge, and on to Burton Salmon, Church Fenton and York. This service was introduced with the opening of the S&K Joint line in 1879, but it was not particularly successful, comprising at the most four trains in each direction daily and it ceased at the end of 1916. Connections to York were given at Doncaster off King's Cross-Leeds trains, and from the 1881 timetable it appears as if there was a through coach (or coaches) between London and York by the 10.10am from King's Cross, taking almost an hour longer than the 10.00am from King's Cross which ran via Selby.

A short-lived Great Northern service to York was from Bradford, via Methley and Milford Junction; this operated only during the summer months of 1876 and 1877.

There was also an emergency route from York to Doncaster via Sherburn, Gascoigne Wood and Selby Canal, joining the 1871 line south of Selby station, and at the time of writing yet another route is being constructed. This is the Selby diversion, designed to avoid the swing bridge at Selby and the subsidence which may occur with the development of the new Selby coalfield.

Midland Railway

On 19 June 1879, a month after the opening of the Swinton & Knottingley Joint line to goods traffic, the Midland Railway requested engine accommodation at York, and in the following month the North Eastern recommended that accommodation should be provided at the new shed at the north end of York station. However, this does not appear to have been implemented and the Midland engines were housed in one of the three roundhouses at the south end.

The Midland was quick to take advantage of the opening of the Swinton & Knottingley line to passenger traffic on 1 July 1879 and by 1881 there were eight trains in each direction daily between York and Sheffield. By the turn of the century this had risen to 10 trains a day, most of them being through between York, Birmingham and Bristol. Exceptions were the 6.05pm arrival at York, which missed Sheffield and called at Masborough, and the 9.38am arrival at York which ran forward to Newcastle, with a through coach for Edinburgh. In the opposite direction the Midland coaches returned as the 12.17pm from Newcastle to Sheffield, which left Darlington at 1.05pm and covered the 44.1 miles to York in 43min.

Above: **At one time East Coast trains were often worked by Stirling singles and this view shows No 95 about to leave York, with the old Locomotive Yard signalbox in the distance. The photograph must have been taken prior to 1897 when No 95 received a domed boiler.** *Author's collection*

Above right: **The GN 4-4-0 engines also worked main line expresses south of York, such as No 1398 passing Milepost 1 about 1910.** *S. Ellingworth*

Right: **GN Atlantic No 1447 was chosen for the trials carried out between Newcastle and Edinburgh in early LNER days, for which it received a cut-down cab. It was a York engine and as No 4447 remained there until July 1943, when it was transferred to the Southern Area in exchange for an 'A7' 4-6-2T. In the 1920s it continued on its main line duties but later it worked with the York based 'D49s' on trains to Scarborough etc.** *Real Photographs*

In the summer months the 9.30am York to Sheffield started back at Scarborough, and the 4.42pm from Sheffield continued to Scarborough at 5.55pm from York. The Newcastle and Scarborough trains were re-engined at York with NER locomotives, although numerous Midland engines worked through to Scarborough on excursions and special trains.

Although the Midland had powers to reach York by two other routes (see Table) these were not exercised. However, the Midland was one of the two companies (the other was the Great Northern) which worked its own goods traffic to York, and even in British Railways days the London, Midland Region engines seen on goods workings at York were almost invariably from former Midland sheds.

The passenger engines stationed at York in Midland days were originally of the 2-4-0 type, later replaced by Class 2P, 3P and 4P 4-4-0s, with 0-6-0s of various types on the freight workings; those allocated to York carried a 27 shed plate but this was changed to 19F from January 1935. The

LMS period brought Stanier 4-6-0 and 2-8-0 engines to York, and in World War 2 they were joined by the Garratts, which continued to appear until BR days.

After the Grouping of 1923 the York-based LMS engines from the Midland section were moved across the main line to share the one-time locomotive works boiler shop with the engines from the Lancashire & Yorkshire section. This building had become an engine shed about 1909, but in 1932 it was closed as a running shed and the LMS engines moved back across the main line to the South shed, this time using the straight shed which had started life as the Great North of England shed. In between it had been used by the

Great Northern engines. The LMS engines concerned were 4-4-0 Nos 400, 401, 402, 563, 727, 728, 729, 1091 and 0-6-0 3715.

Lancashire & Yorkshire Railway

Next to reach York was the Lancashire & Yorkshire from Normanton on 1 May 1884, with powers to work passenger traffic only, using Midland metals to Altofts Junction and the NER thence to York. This arrangement was verified by an Agreement dated 5 February 1886, and cattle traffic was also permitted under arrangements made in 1896. In 1902, at the height of the summer, the L&Y worked eight trains to and from York, two of which were extended to, and started back from, Scarborough; however, it is not clear if L&Y engines worked through, although the

coaches certainly did. The 2.28pm from York to Liverpool started from Newcastle at 12.30pm, and the 11.10am from Liverpool (York 1.45pm to 2.12pm) ran through to Newcastle (arrive 3.51pm) North Eastern engines worked these trains between York and Newcastle.

For many years the Lancashire & Yorkshire trains were worked by 4-4-0s of various types, followed by the Aspinall Atlantics and the Hughes 4-6-0s. These larger engines became a familiar sight at York; the Atlantics disappeared around 1930, although the 4-6-0 engines continued to appear at York until 1951, when their end was marked by a special train from Blackpool to York, worked by No 50455. The ubiquitous 2-4-2T engines also appeared at York, and 0-6-0 engines were to be seen on the many L&Y excursions from Lancashire and the West Riding of Yorkshire to Scarborough.

The Lancashire & Yorkshire paid the standard charge of £25 per annum for each engine stationed at York and these engines were allowed to use the NER turntable free of charge; visiting L&Y engines were charged 6d per time to turn! Water was charged at one shilling a tank, coal at 12s 6d a ton, and lighting-up was one shilling a time.

Top left: **The other large GN Atlantic at York was No 4424, seen arriving at York on a train from Scarborough.** *Author's collection*

Centre left: **The south end of York station in August 1937. Note that Queen Street shed (which housed the LMS engines) has been closed. The engine is 'K3' No 4005, probably deputising for a Gresley Pacific on this heavy East Coast train.** *Real Photographs*

Bottom left: **For working the 10.23am to Bournemouth the Great Central stationed 'Director' No 438 *Worsley-Taylor* at York. The location is once again Holgate platforms, but prior to the removal of the bank behind the down platform to allow reception sidings to be constructed.** *S. Ellingworth*

Below: **Sheffield based 'Director' class engines continued to work into York in LNER days, such as No 5436 *Sir Berkeley Sheffield*.** *C. Ord*

Specimen figures (for 1897) are:

	£ s d
2,504 tanks of water at 1/-	125-4-0
Stabling 3 engines at £25	75-0-0
1,529 engines turned at 6d	38-4-6
138 tons of coal at 12/6d per ton	86-5-0
Lighting-up: 987 at 1/-	49-7-0
	374-0-6

Great Eastern Railway

The Great Eastern started working through to York from Doncaster on 1 November 1892; there were three trains in each direction to and from the Eastern Counties and London (Liverpool Street) at 10.25am, 12.52pm and 4.37pm from York. In addition there was a dining car express boat train from York (dep 3.50pm) to Harwich (Parkeston Quay) giving an arrival at Hook of Holland at 5.05am the following morning. Great Eastern arrivals from Liverpool Street were at 2.15pm, 4.22pm, and 9.52pm, and from Parkeston Quay at 12.55pm.

All engine and carriage accommodation, and services, at York were provided by the North Eastern and charged to the Great Eastern.

The Great Eastern engines noted at York were James Holden's 2-2-2, 4-2-2 and 2-4-0 types, the latter in their original and rebuilt 'Humpty Dumpy' form and also after rebuilding further to 4-4-0s. Finally 'Claud' 4-4-0s worked to York in LNER days before 'B17' 4-6-0s appeared.

About 1920 the Great Eastern decided to withdraw its engine from York and arrangements were made with the North Eastern for the latter to work the 10.25am to Lincoln and the 2.36pm return, getting back to York at 4.30pm. North Eastern 4-4-0 and 4-4-2 engines were used on this working, which continued for many years.

London & North Western Railway

From 1 July 1893 the London & North Western Railway extended three of its Liverpool-Leeds trains to York and worked them with its own engines. In the summer season two trains were extended further to Scarborough (1.20pm and 5.20pm from Leeds) but it is not clear if the engines worked through to the coast, although

Below: **Most long-distance trains passing through York were East Coast expresses made up of ECJS vehicles, but a train of Great Western stock worked through on the Barry-Newcastle train — down one day and up the next. This is the up train about to leave for Sheffield behind Class R 4-4-0 No 2101.**
Crown Copyright, National Railway Museum, York

Top right: **The Great Eastern worked its trains into York with a variety of engines, including this Holden single which was probably out-stationed at York. The engine is standing at the South shed with the large signal gantry in the background controlling trains entering the station from the south.** *Author's collection*

Right: **Great Eastern No 1039 was the last to be built of the numerous 'T19' class and appeared in 1897. Note that the signals on the gantry have been changed to the new North Eastern standard with the spectacle in line with the arm.** *Author's collection*

there are recollections of 2-2-2 *Eunomia* and 2-4-0 *Belted Will* being regular visitors to Scarborough at about that time. Similarly the 2.23pm York-Liverpool started back at Scarborough at 1.20pm, and the 4.35pm York-Liverpool left Scarborough at 3.25pm. E. L. Ahrons mentions 2-2-2 *Saracen* on the Leeds-York trains but so far I have been unable to locate any views taken on the NER of the three engines mentioned. The LNWR locomotives last worked to York on 31 December 1904.

Great Central Railway

The final 'foreigner' to reach York was the Great Central on 13 March 1899, with three trains in each direction daily to Sheffield (Victoria) and beyond, at 9.25am, 2.47pm and 4.45pm from York. The 9.25am Breakfast Car express to Bournemouth started at Newcastle at 7.05am, and in the opposite direction the 10.47am from Bournemouth reached York at 7.40pm and worked forward to Newcastle at 7.55pm; both up and down trains were worked by North Eastern

Left: Larger boilers were fitted to 21 of the 'T19' class and as it was pitched 12in higher than on the original engines it gave them a humped appearance, leading to their nickname of 'Humpty-Dumpty'. This is No 770 at the South shed. The class also worked into York in their final form as 4-4-0s (LNER Class D13). *Author's collection*

Centre left: The 'Claud' 4-4-0s worked into York from Lincoln on the Harwich Boat Train, notably No 8874 of Class D15 which was also seen at Scarborough. A 1957 RCTS rail-tour brought No 62571 of Class D16/3 to York and it was photographed near Chaloners Whin, heading south. *C. Ord*

Bottom left: LMS trains from Sheffield (Midland) brought various types of 4-4-0s to York, including No 711 carrying a Saltley shed-plate. The driver and fireman are carrying out 'Loco Duties' at Queen Street shed. *Real Photographs*

Below: I have never seen a photograph of a London & North Western engine at York when they worked in from Leeds between 1893 and 1904, but E. L. Ahrons (in his *Locomotive and Train Working in the Latter Part of the 19th Century*) recalls that 2-2-2 No 1 *Saracen* was stationed at Leeds for working to York. *LPC*

Bottom: The Lancashire & Yorkshire worked many of its trains with 4-4-0 engines, such as No 1099 passing Holgate Platforms. *L&GRP, courtesy David & Charles*

engines north of York and ran via Stockton and Sunderland.

The usual charge of £25 was made for stabling a Great Central engine at York, and the NER also charged for accommodating and shunting Great Central coaches, and for examining those working through York. The GC used its own staff to wash, clean, and light the coaches, and to supply footwarmers.

On 1 May 1906 a through train commenced running between Barry Island and Newcastle, using Great Central and Great Western rolling stock and guards. This was operated by the Great Western, Great Central and North Eastern, and the North Eastern agreed to engine the trains between Sheffield and York at 9d per engine mile. This working was a long day for the York footplate crew, who first worked the 5.55am York to Darlington slow, and the 8.35am return, before leaving for Sheffield at 11.40am and getting back at 4.35pm. They were relieved on arrival back at York and by the time they had signed off they had worked an 11hr 10min day. Prior to World War 1 the Great Central engine based at York was an Atlantic, but subsequently a 'Director' was used, notably No 438 *Worsley Taylor*.

The Great Central did not work its own goods

Above: **Later the Hughes 4-6-0s were frequent visitors in both their original and rebuilt versions. No 10426 was photographed on the turntable at Queen Street, with the former No 2 Erecting Shop in the background.** *Author's collection*

Right: **In BR days 'Patriots' and 'Royal Scots' reached York, one of the former being No 45517 of Bank Hall shed.** *E. Sanderson*

trains through to York but handed them over to the North Eastern at Milford Junction, 14½ miles south of York. Where there was no return working the GC engine then ran light to Mexborough, and conversely engines were sent out from Mexborough to work trains from Milford Junction to Great Central destinations. A Mexborough engine actually performed the Great Central shunting duties at Milford Junction.

East Coast Joint Stock

In November 1855 an agreement was signed whereby the Great Northern, North Eastern, North British, Edinburgh & Glasgow, and Scottish Central companies 'being mutually desirous of facilitating the traffic along the East Coast route and of establishing a united system for the working and management of through traffic' decided to work together for their mutual benefit. This led five years later to the suggestion that there should be a common stock of vehicles for East Coast use, and before 1860 was out the Great Northern, North Eastern and North British had agreed to a pool of 50 coaches and brakevans, with the cost of £13,450 divided between them in proportion to the mileage.

The vehicles, all four-wheel, were put into traffic in 1861 and until the end of 1922 ECJS coaches were a familiar sight on the main line. At first the Great Northern was the dominant partner, designing and building most of the stock at its Doncaster works, and it was not until 1895 that the North Eastern was allowed to provide vehicles built at its York carriage works. Bogie coaches were built from 1893.

Finished in the teak livery of the Great Northern the East Coast vehicles displayed the arms of England and Scotland on the side panels together with (on some vehicles) the ECJS device. Under LNER ownership, with the three companies under common control, the teak livery was retained but the arms disappeared: at first a letter J suffix was added to the ECJS number, but later this was dispensed with and a figure 1 prefix was used instead.

Company	Between	Distance	Agreement	Class of Traffic	Exercised	Remarks
Great Northern	Knottingley-York	19M 55c*	25-11-1848 25-11-1850	All	Coaching	—
Great Northern	Shaftholme Junc-York	28M 0c*	15-3-1864	All	All	Commenced 2-1-1871
Midland	Altofts Junc-York	23M 41c*	30-10-1874	All	Not exercised	—
Midland	Ferrybridge Junc-York	19M 15c*	30-10-1874	All	Coaching, goods and livestock	Commenced 7-1879
Midland	Methley (Midland Junc)-York	23M 5c*	30-10-1874	All	Not exercised	—
Lancashire & Yorkshire	Altofts Junc-York	23M 41c*	5-2-1886	Coaching and cattle	Coaching and cattle	Commenced 1-5-1884
Great Eastern	Shaftholme Junc-York	28M 0c	24-3-1893	Coaching	Coaching	Commenced 1-11-1892
London & North Western	Leeds-York	25M 29c	17-6-1893	Through: coaching — local passengers only	Through: coaching — local passengers only	Commenced 1-7-1893 Ceased 31-12-1904
Great Central	Ferrybridge Junc-York	19M 15c	1-12-1898	Coaching	Coaching	Commenced 15-3-1899

*Distance quoted is to passenger station. Goods station 1M 29c additional

Below: The LMS 'Crab' 2-6-0s were also frequent visitors, and even in their original red livery and 13xxx numbers could be seen working through to Scarborough. This view of No 42846 of Saltley was taken in September 1956 when it was setting off on a Sheffield slow. *Author*

Development of Freight Services

York, of course, was not an industrial city, although it had numerous small industrial concerns mainly concerned with supplying the requirements of the city and the surrounding area. However, two industries did stand way above all the others, namely flour milling (largely because of the confluence of the rivers Ouse and Foss), and the manufacture of confectionery. Thus in 1923 the greatest bulk traffic despatched from York was flour and bran, amounting to 79,972 tons, and the greatest 'Carted & Delivered' traffic was confectionery at 14,976 tons, largely from Messrs Rowntree's factory on Haxby Road, although J. Terry & Sons Ltd (with no rail connection) was another large manufacturer with national distribution. The second largest bulk traffic was, surprisingly, scrap iron and steel (presumably from the railway carriage and wagon shops) at 18,878 tons, whilst 9,959 tons of railway wagons were despatched OOW (on own wheels). Being at the centre of a large agricultural area York handled 7,884 wagons of cattle in 1923 — second only to Newcastle in the North Eastern Area of the LNER.

Most of the city's goods traffic was handled at the goods station and warehouse in Leeman Road, with some bulk traffics dealt with at Foss Islands, but with the decline in traffic British Rail handed over the Leeman Road building to National Carriers Ltd in 1972 and concentrated traffic at Foss Islands. However, within a few years NCL vacated the Leeman Road building and it was taken over as a store and workshop for the National Railway Museum on the opposite side of Leeman Road. The building is now known as The Peter Allen Building and it houses the Museum's reserve collection and items undergoing restoration. The building was formally named by Sir Peter himself on 24 October 1979.

The NER Working Timetable for January 1861 consisted of only 20 pages, but by that time numerous goods and mineral trains were shown in the Darlington-York table; these included a 'Meat Train' at 3.55am from Newcastle, stopping only at Darlington and Thirsk and due in York at 8.30am; an 'Aberdeen Express Goods' leaving Newcastle at 9.30am and due in York at 2.15pm, again with Darlington and Thirsk stops; and a 'Fish Train' leaving Newcastle at 3.10pm and arriving at York at 7.40pm with three stops. There were numerous mineral trains, mainly 'Coke for Normanton' or 'GN Coal', although one train, the 2.30pm from Sherburn, due in York at 7.00pm, is described as 'Coote's Train'. Thomas Coote was a St Ives coal merchant who, in November 1856, agreed to supply not less than 78,000 tons of coal a year from Peterborough to 50 stations on the Eastern Counties Railway, and over its section of the journey the North Eastern Railway agreed to carry this coal at $\frac{1}{2}$d per ton per mile, with a reduced rate after 50,000 tons had been carried. In 1872 Stockton & Darlington Section engines were working through from Shildon to Hexthorpe Sidings (Doncaster) on train loads of Durham coke for the Manchester, Sheffield & Lincolnshire company, and by 1874 this traffic warranted three trains a day through York.

On the Scarborough branch in 1861 there were four trains daily for Scarborough — one cattle, one goods and two coal, with one goods for Whitby, whilst on the Market Weighton branch one goods and one coal sufficed. Between York and Starbeck there was one coal train and two 'Passenger and Goods', the first mixed train of the day at 6.30am from York took 70min for the $18\frac{1}{4}$-mile journey as it stopped only at Knaresborough, but the 12.50pm from York took two hours due to stopping at every station. Even 75 years later (1936) the Scarborough branch required only one through goods, one pick-up goods, and one mineral train each day!

The greatest changes occurred on the main line towards the end of the 19th century when express goods services were developed; such trains running between Berwick and Normanton were designated 'SWB' (Special White Board) trains for the simple reason that they carried two white boards indicating their status, one at the foot of

Above: The offices fronting the Goods Warehouse, photographed in 1908, with an unusual double-sided weigh-house in the right foreground. The warehouse is now used as an annexe to the National Railway Museum (on the opposite side of Leeman Road) and is known as The Peter Allen Building.
Crown Copyright, National Railway Museum, York

Above right: During its existence the North Eastern Railway relied extensively on 0-6-0 engines for working its goods and mineral traffic. Many of the Fletcher engines were scrapped in the first decade of the century when numerous modern engines were built to the designs of Wilson Worsdell. One engine involved was this short-wheelbase 0-6-0, No 657 of Class 93, built in 1867 and scrapped in 1908. It was photographed at York shed about 1906, with the up ticket platform in the background. A similar engine, sold to a Northumberland colliery company in 1908, existed until 1959. *LPC*

Right: Also used extensively on goods work were the various engines collected together under Class 398. No 1451, on a lengthy up goods, takes the goods lines at Poppleton Junction, with the Harrogate branch curving away on the left. *H. L. Salmon*

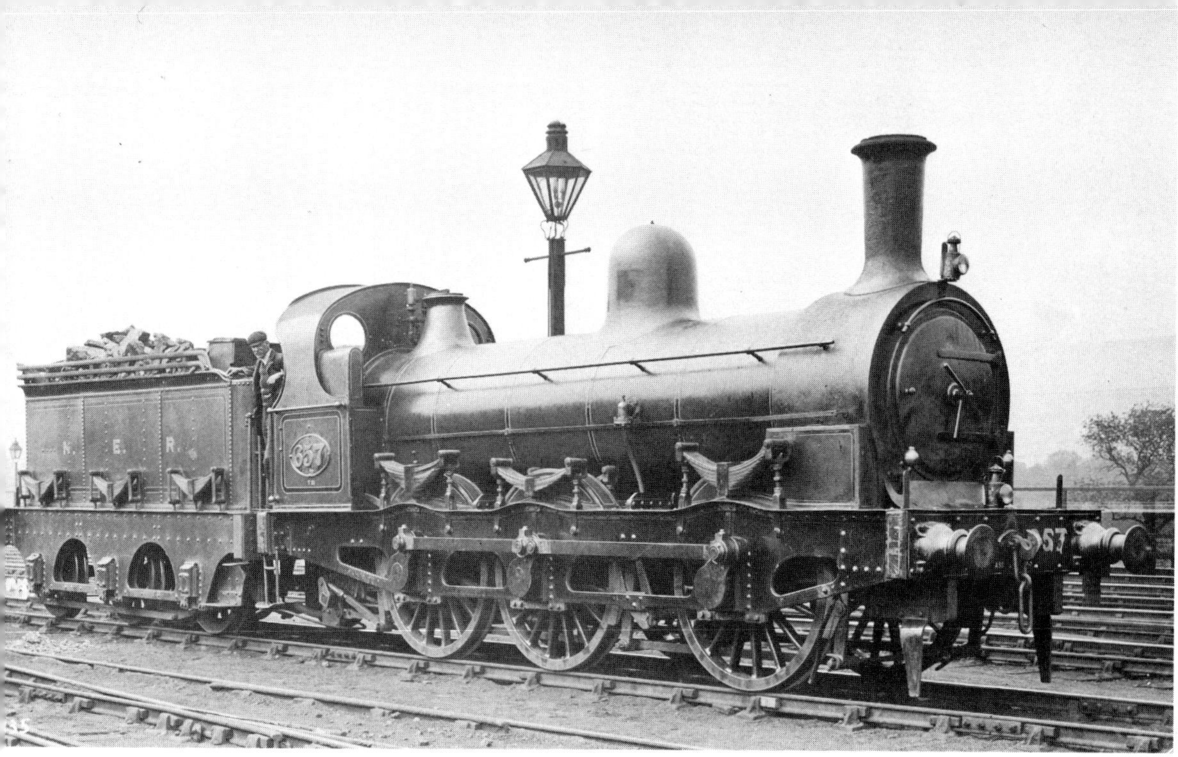
N. E. R.
657

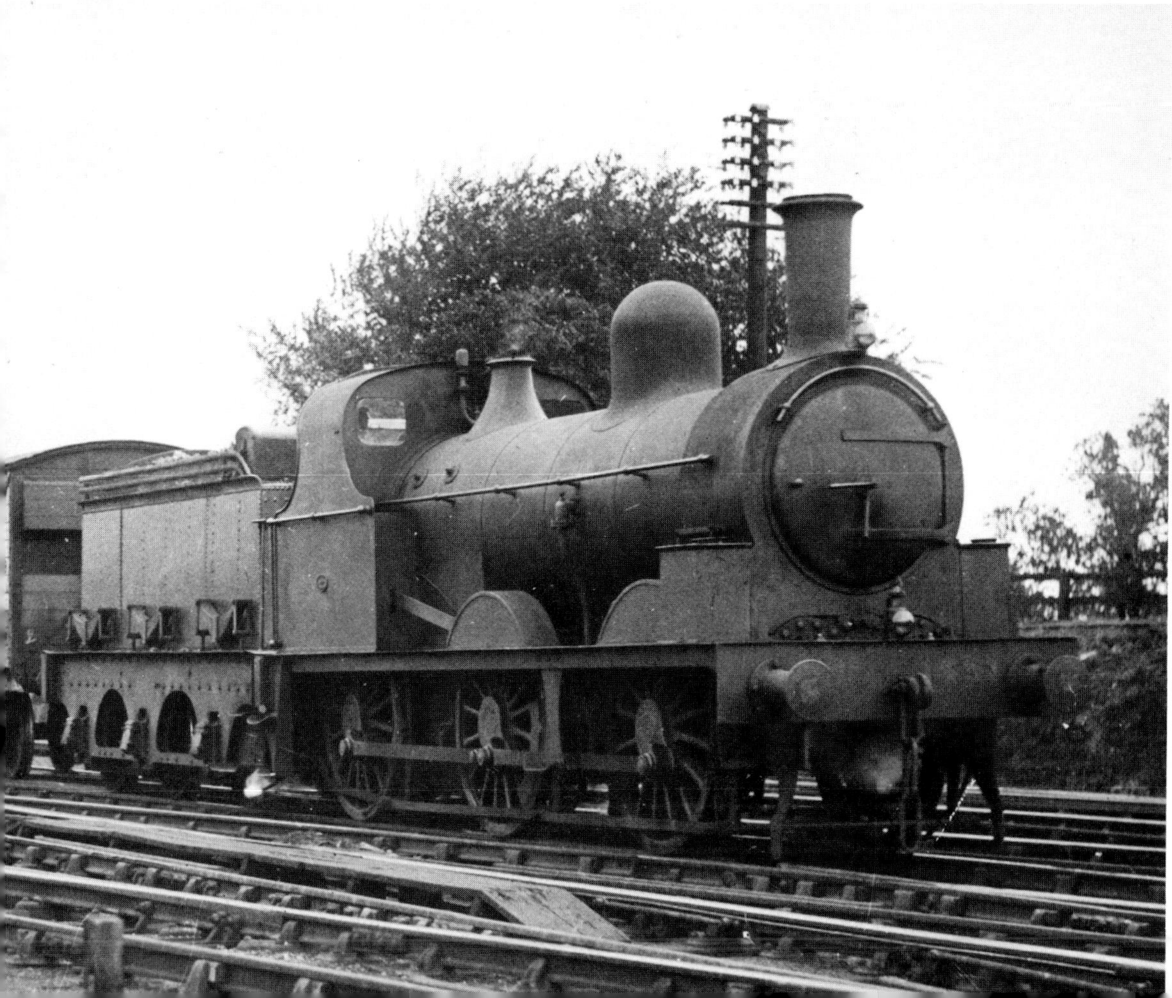

Left: T. W. Worsdell's first design of 0-6-0 was intended for goods work when the first engine appeared in 1886, but subsequently many were fitted with Westinghouse brake (and later vacuum brake) for use on express goods and passenger trains. In this form they proved a very useful mixed traffic engine. No 1808 was a York engine and was photographed on the Up Main at the south end of the station. *W. L. Good*

Centre left: With their 4ft 7$\frac{1}{4}$in wheels the 'P' and 'P1' engines were intended for use solely on goods work and they were not normally fitted with automatic brakes. A dirty 'P1' engine, No 2068, is heading south from York Yard on the Up Leeds line. The leading five vehicles are lime washed cattle wagons, followed by a rake of 20-ton hopper wagons. The signals are off for a down goods into York Yard, and an up train on the Doncaster line has a clear distant. *H. L. Salmon*

Below: The large boilered 'P2' engines were never plentiful around York but No 525 was for long a York engine, seen here on a lengthy train of mineral wagons at South Points. *H. L. Salmon*

Left: The Class S 4-6-0 engines were designed initially for express passenger work but were soon found to be more satisfactory on goods trains. This engine, No 2002, was the second engine of the class, built in 1899. *W. L. Good*

Below: York Atlantic No 2163 on an up goods at Poppleton Junction. *H. L. Salmon*

Left: A sugar beet factory was opened at Poppleton Junction in 1926 and purchased two 0-4-0ST locomotives from Andrew Barclay, Sons & Co Ltd (AB 1884 of 1926 and 1897 of 1927). During the sugar beet season — September to February — the crop was received by rail and road and this 1943 view shows wagons awaiting unloading. *BR*

the chimney and one at the centre of the buffer-beam. They were similarly designated in the Working Timetable, with special instructions for the bell signals to be given for these trains. One train was booked to run from Newcastle to York, via the High Level Bridge and the Team Valley route, in two hours, with one brief stop at Darlington for inspection — and that in 1893!

Although flows of goods and mineral traffic from County Durham and the heavily industrialised Teesside area joined at North-allerton the extensive marshalling yard planned for Northallerton did not materialise and traffic was sorted at Thirsk for destinations beyond York. Thus York did not require extensive yards as much of the traffic was through from Scotland to London and the south, or from Thirsk, Darlington and Newport to the industrial centres of York-shire, Lancashire and the Midlands. Consequently York's main function was to sort the wagons for the pick-up goods trains serving the various branches, although Scarborough did warrant a through goods each morning until well into BR days. What shunting there was had to be carried out in up and down yards on both sides of the line between North Junction (later York Yard South) and Severus Junction (later York Yard North), and in Branches Yard (between Leeman Road and North Junction). Trains using these yards did not pass through the station and, in fact, at busy periods freight traffic of any kind was banned from passing through the station. Dringhouses Yard, on the up side south of the station, was constructed in 1915/6 for the increased traffic brought about by World War 1.

In LNER days No 1 Braked Goods, such as the well-known 3.40pm King's Cross-Niddrie, were designated 'To take precedence over all trains except East Coast Passenger Trains' and in 1932 this train was allowed 106min from York to New-castle (80 miles) with no stops. In the up direction the 10.40am No 1 Braked Meat from Aberdeen (5.23pm from Newcastle) was allowed only 101min from Newcastle to York. Another notable train was the 6.19pm fish train from Heaton, which was booked to leave Newcastle Central at 6.53pm and run to York in 110min. This was rostered to be worked by a Heaton Atlantic or 4-6-0 and warranted the following footnote in the WTT: 'Frequently runs in two portions. Will run in front of 7.00pm Mail if it can leave with a margin of 3min. Stops at Darlington by signal when necessary for traffic purposes in which case the train will run a few minutes later to York. Must not be shunted between Newcastle and York for the Mail to pass; arrives at and departs from York fish-stage (Clifton Sidings). When cannot leave Newcastle at booked time the journey from New-castle to York must be run in 100min'. The engine returned on a parcels train at 12.30am from York.

In NER and LNER days many of these main line freight trains were worked by the top passenger engines, such as Raven Atlantics and Gresley Pacifics. In North Eastern days the 1.45pm Aberdeen-King's Cross fish train was worked from Newcastle by the York Atlantic which had gone north on the Swansea-Newcastle express (York dep 4.42pm), but in the 1930s this turn was worked by Gateshead shed, often using the water-tube boiler engine No 10000. This involved

Above left: **The Great Northern worked its own goods trains between Doncaster and York and this view shows 2-4-0 No 293A heading south near South Points. The engine was built by the Yorkshire Engine Co in 1868 and was to Stirling's first design for the GN.** *Author's collection*

Left: **The Great Northern 4-4-0s stationed at York took their turn on goods workings, such as No 1386N heading for Doncaster about 1924.** *H. L. Salmon*

Below: **In the early 1920s the North Eastern was allotted some of the WD 2-8-0 engines built for the Railway Operating Department. The LNER later purchased a number of these engines from the Government and of the 44 purchased in 1928 five were allocated to York, including No 6617. The photograph was taken outside the old Great North of England shed with the engine newly painted in LNER colours.** *LPC*

working the 10.05am from York between New-castle and Edinburgh, and then the Aberdeen fish right through to York, with a change of men at Newcastle; the final leg from York back home to Newcastle was on a sleeping car train from London to Scotland. The Aberdeen fish was actually signalled as an Express Passenger train.

Most fitted freights succumbed with World War 2 but were rapidly reintroduced in 1945, with greater use being made of the up yard at Dringhouses, particularly during the night. By 1962 the yard was receiving some 850 wagons a night from the north-east and these were sorted into approximately 30 trains bound for the industrial centres of the Midlands and the southern and western parts of the country. In fact Dringhouses became the first marshalling yard in the country to deal exclusively with fully fitted braked express goods trains.

During 1961 the yard was converted into a 'hump' yard and at the same time the existing sidings were lengthened and nine additional sidings provided on the east side. An elevated

control room was built at the north end of the yard, with the layout depicted on an illuminated panel so that the operator could run the wagons into the appropriate sidings and at the same time control their speed by means of hydraulically operated retarders.

Foss Islands Branch
As early as November 1856 the Lord Mayor of York led a deputation to meet the Directors of the North Eastern Railway to ask for a branch to the cattle market, which was across the city from the station and the goods yard. However, it was 17 years before the North Eastern decided to go ahead with the branch, and another seven years before the line was opened. The Act was obtained on 16 July 1874 and the contract for making the line was awarded to Walter Scott of Newcastle on 11 October 1877 at a figure of £37,889. The branch, 1 mile 52 chains long, was formally opened on 8 December 1879 but not fully opened until 1 January 1880.

The branch left the Scarborough line at a new

Left: The most useful engines to be stationed at York were the 'B16' 4-6-0s and from 28 March 1943 all 69 of the class were allocated to York shed. One of the class, No 925, had been damaged beyond repair in the air raid on York in 1942. Here No 61451 trundles towards York Yard South box on the Down Scarborough Goods line. The train has no brake van but will probably have a tail lamp, or a red flag, hanging on the drawhook of the last wagon. Much of the area in the photograph is now a car park for the National Railway Museum. *Author's collection*

Top right: One of the engines rebuilt to 'B16/2', No 61455, approaches York from the south on a train of empty bogie bolster wagons. The track with buffer stops, on the up side, is the shunting neck at the south end of Dringhouses Yard. *Author's collection*

Right: Most through goods and mineral trains avoided the station by running via York Yard, but one train which had to pass through the station each day was the Gascoigne Wood-Scarborough mineral train, seen here in charge of 'D49' *The Badsworth* in July 1954. *Author*

Below: Some of the 'QG' 0-0-0 engines were stationed at Selby, including No 63348, taking the Selby and Doncaster line at Chaloners Whin Junction. *C. Ord*

junction at Burton Lane, 1 mile 4 chains from York station, and swung round the eastern outskirts of the city to terminate outside the Walls near Walmgate Bar. Over the years there has been much industrial development along the branch, which eventually served the gasworks, the Corporation electricity works, Messrs H. I. Rowntree & Co Ltd (cocoa and chocolate works), Henry Leetham & Sons Ltd (millers), the NER Laundry, various coal merchants, and the Derwent Valley Light Railway.

The Foss Islands branch, being almost wholly single line, was worked in North Eastern days with a Staff and four Tickets, the working being controlled by the signalman at Burton Lane and the Staff Attendant at Foss Islands. When the Staff Attendant was not on duty only one train could work on the branch, with the driver in possession of the Staff; if two trains were necessary then the Staff Attendant had to be brought on duty specially by arrangement with the York Yardmaster.

The single line actually extended from Burton Lane's down starting signal, and between Burton Lane Junction and this signal was double track with a loop on the down side to accommodate the halt established in 1927 for workpeople and parties of visitors to Rowntree's works. Trains leaving the halt ran on to the down line and then on to the up line to arrive at Burton Lane ready to join the up Scarborough line. A large amount of miscellaneous freight traffic is still forwarded to and from Messrs Rowntree's works via their internal rail system, which connects with the Foss Islands branch immediately south of the halt. The halt was originally named Rowntree's Cocoa Works and this was displayed on a typical NER

enamelled nameboard, but it later became Rowntree's Halt.

Locomotives operated by the various concerns on the Foss Islands branch included steam, electric and diesel; York Power Station had two four-wheel overhead-wire electric locomotives by Metropolitan-Vickers and Kerr, Stuart, and for a time Leetham's Flour Mills had a vertical boiler Atkinson-Walker shunter. This was purchased in 1927 and subsequently went to the War Department at Eskmeals, in Cumberland. York Gas Works had three 0-4-0ST engines by Peckett, Bagnall and Hudswell, Clarke, and Rowntree Ltd (now Rowntree-Mackintosh) had five 0-4-0ST at various times; these were by Barclay, Hudswell, Clarke, two by Hunslet Engine Co, and one of uncertain parentage. A change to diesel traction commenced in 1958 and four Ruston & Hornsby locomotives — one diesel-electric and three diesel-mechanical — were purchased, although one of the latter later moved to Rowntree's Newcastle factory.

North Sea gas and the gigantic power stations in South Yorkshire have eliminated most of the coal traffic on the Foss Islands branch, although the closure of Leeman Road depots in 1966, and Leeman Road goods station in 1972, meant the concentration of York's goods traffic at Foss Islands, together with a special sand traffic for a local glassworks. The Derwent Valley's yard at Layerthorpe also handles bulk traffics, which traverse the Foss Islands branch.

Derwent Valley Light Railway
The Derwent Valley Light Railway was formed as a result of local landowners requiring transport for their agricultural produce, and it served an

Above left: **A coke train off the Midland line approaching York with Holbeck '4F' 0-6-0 No 43968 in charge in 1954.** *Author*

Above: **Newport WD 2-8-0 No 90091 waits for the road at the south end of York station in August 1955, with a load of steel from Teesside.** *Author*

Right: **York Yard South new box (formerly North Junction) photographed from the footbridge on the right of way from Leeman Road to Holgate Road — known as 'the cinder path'. The bridge in the foreground joins the carriage works (left) and the wagon works (right); the sugar beet factory is in the background.** *E. Sanderson*

Below right: **Installing retarders at the north end of Dringhouses Yard in 1961. The control cabin is under construction in the left background.** *E. Sanderson*

Top left: A telephoto lens view of the south end of Dringhouses Yard, with a train of empty mineral wagons passing on the Up Leeds line. *E. Sanderson*

Centre left: 9F No 92089 passing Milepost 1 on an up goods. *E. Sanderson*

Left: An up express headed by two 'B1' 4-6-0s overhauls sister engine No 61321 of Darlington plodding south at the site of South Points box, with the entrance to Dringhouses Yard on the right.
E. Sanderson

Top: Two engines from the Southern Region, Nos D6577 and D6584, arrive at Skelton sidings on the 'Blue Circle' Cliffe-Uddingston cement train in January 1962. These sidings — six Up Reception and six Down Reception — were installed in World War 2 (but have now been lifted). At the same time a new bridge over the River Ouse carried a much needed down Independent to get freight traffic moving northwards without waiting for a path on the main line. *BR*

Above: 'B1' No 61084 standing at Rowntree's Halt platform, with the chocolate works in the background. *Author's collection*

area of rich farmland to the east of the York-Selby section of the East Coast main line.

It diverged from the Foss Islands branch at Hallfield Road Junction and after crossing the British Rail boundary ran for 16 miles, first east and then south parallel to the River Derwent, to join the Selby-Market Weighton line at Cliff Common. Attractive single-platform stations were provided to handle the passenger traffic, with the company's headquarters at Layerthorpe station; unfortunately the station was in an out-of-way location on the east side of York and the passenger service, which commenced on 21 July 1913, was withdrawn from 1 September 1926, but the goods traffic continued for many years. From 1 January 1965 the line was steadily cut back until on 28 September 1981 the whole of the line was closed and the company retained only the tracks in the yard at Layerthorpe. This was because the operation of the actual railway was making a loss, with by far the largest amount of the company's income coming from the rents of the various installations handling coal and oil etc at Layerthorpe.

The only steam locomotive owned by the DV was a Sentinel shunter (Works No S6076) purchased in 1925 for £1,400. Until then the company had hired locomotives from the NER and LNER and at the Annual General Meeting held at York on 18 March 1927 the Chairman (Lord Deramore) reported that the acquisition of the Sentinel had reduced the cost of engine power

Right: An early RCTS rail-tour has traversed the Derwent Valley Light Railway and is heading for York station along the Foss Islands Branch. It has just passed under Heworth Green and is passing the former NER Laundry, with wagons of coal for the boilers in the Laundry siding. *C. Ord*

Centre right: For many years the clean linen was delivered to the Royal Station Hotel and the station by this Vulcan van and it was a familiar sight in Tea Room Square at the station.
Crown Copyright, National Railway Museum, York

Bottom right: The Foss Islands branch served the local electricity works where shunting was carried out by two electric locomotives: this one, CEA NEB YORK No 1, was built by Metropolitan-Vickers and was photographed in 1961. *B. Webb*

Above left: With the closure of Branches Yard and the removal of the crossings at the north end of the station the empty vans for the Rowntree's traffic had to be marshalled in Dringhouses Yard and worked through the station by a diesel-electric shunter.
E. Sanderson

Left: 'J27' No 65885 is entering the single line section of the Foss Islands branch and passing over the set of hold-up points giving access to the double track section to Burton Lane box. *P. J. Lynch*

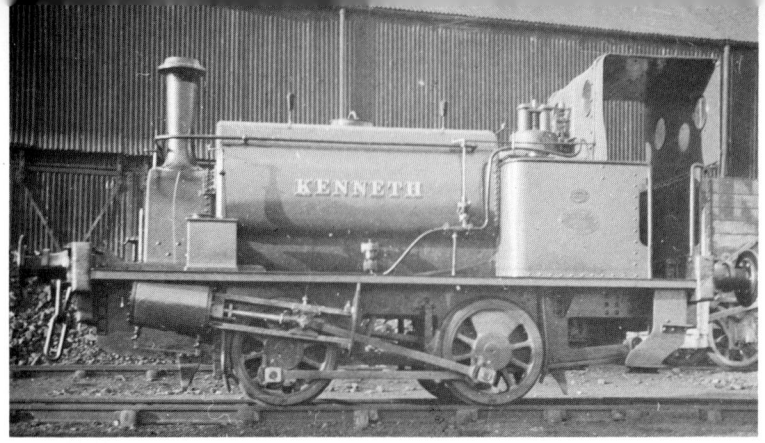

Left: **York United Gas Co owned 0-4-0ST** *Kenneth,* **built by Hudswell, Clarke in 1895.** *Author's collection*

Centre left: **At the formal opening ceremony of the Derwent Valley Light Railway on 19 July 1913 the first train was 'released' when Lady Deramore cut a ribbon at Layerthorpe station. The inaugural train included two open wagons (with seats) in which Lord and Lady Deramore rode (third and second from left respectively) with members of the official party.**
Author's collection

Below: **In 1977 the Derwent Valley line between Layerthorpe and Dunnington was used by a steam hauled service work by** *Joem,* **a former 'J72' 0-6-0T. This is the inaugural train standing at Layerthorpe awaiting the arrival of the Lord Mayor on 4 May 1977.** *Author*

Right: **Also in 1977 the Derwent Valley line saw LNWR 2-4-0** *Hardwicke,* **photographed on the Foss Islands branch just south of the Heworth Green overbridge.**
E. Sanderson

from £2,800 in 1924 to £1,200 in 1926. However, because of a decrease in traffic the DV had to dispose of its Sentinel locomotive in 1927 and it was sold to Thos Summerson & Sons Ltd, of Albert Hill Foundry in Darlington where it remained until scrapped in 1970.

After the Sentinel had gone the DV resumed hiring locomotives for the goods traffic until it purchased its own diesel locomotives in 1969; these were formerly BR Nos 2245 and 2298 and cost £5,060 the pair. For its passenger traffic the DV purchased two Ford buses on rail wheels, with bodies by C. Roe Ltd of Leeds, the cost being £1,070. On the withdrawal of the passenger service in 1926 these two cars, which were designed to run back to back with the leading car hauling the other, were sold to the County Donegal Railway and modified to suit its 3ft gauge. On the Derwent Valley the rail-buses could be used singly if traffic was so light that only one vehicle was required, but as driving controls were

fitted at only one end this meant turning the bus at each end of its run and for this light turntables were installed at York (Layerthorpe) and Skipwith.

In the final timetable only one train a week ran through from York to Cliff Common — the 8.45am from Layerthorpe on Mondays, returning at 9.50am; the purpose of the outward train was to allow passengers from DV stations to join a LNER Market Weighton-Selby train, Monday being market day in Selby. Also for their benefit was the 4.15pm from Cliff Common to York on Mondays, which ran empty to Cliff Common for this working. All the other trains from York at 8.45am (MX), 12.30pm (SX), 1.20pm (SO), 4.00pm (SO) and 6.00pm (M-S) terminated at Skipwith. The times of the Derwent Valley trains were included in the LNER timetable although it was quite a distance from the main line station at York to the DV station.

The Motive Power Scene

In March 1838 the York & North Midland ordered three locomotives from Robert Stephenson & Co, one to be delivered in six months and the other two in 10 months, but the first, *Lowther,* was not received at York until January 1839. In April 1839 *Lowther* was tried out when 'a large number of respectable inhabitants congregated near the enginehouse on the line between Thief Lane and the viaduct in Holdgate'; the train ran as far as Copmanthorpe 'at a tolerably brisk pace', returning to York some 40 minutes after leaving. Subsequent engines came from Stephenson & Co, Shepherd & Todd, Linton (of Selby), Kitson, Murray & Jackson, Turner & Ogden etc, and by July 1846 the company had 33 engines for passenger trains and 15 for goods traffic. Y&NM engines became NER Nos 245-358 in 1854, when they were mainly of the 2-2-2, 2-4-0, 0-4-2 and 0-6-0 wheel arrangement.

The Great North of England ordered its first two engines in August 1838; these were 'pattern' engines for delivery by 1 February 1839, but the first, *Victoria*, was not completed until June 1839. The GNE purchased its locomotives from Stephenson & Co, Fairbairn, Tayleur etc, and by July 1846 had 16 passenger engines and 21 merchandise engines. The GNE engines carried only names until they were combined with the Newcastle & Darlington Junction engines to form a York & Newcastle numerical list. These were later combined with the engines from other companies to form the York, Newcastle & Berwick list, before becoming NER No 1-244.

Edward Fletcher was appointed Locomotive Engineer of the NER on its formation in 1854 and, as he remained in office until 1882, engines to his designs took over the main line workings into York as the old pre-NER engines were swept away. Alexander McDonnell replaced Fletcher, but his short reign was insufficient to make any great impression on the main line locomotives, and it was not until the appointment of T. W. Worsdell in 1885 that notice began to be taken of the North Eastern's handsome new locomotives,

Below: The oldest engine shed at York was the three-road straight shed at the south end of the station, originating in 1841, probably for the Great North of England Railway and at first accommodating only six engines. For a time it was occupied by the Great Northern engines stationed at York, and in the 1930s by the LMS engines, such as '3P' 4-4-0 No 731. It was demolished in November 1963. The small coaling stage on the right was used to refuel the 'J71' and 'J72' pilot engines. *L. W. Perkins*

Right: There were three individual roundhouses at York South depot; No 1 shed was destroyed by fire in 1921 but the other two — roofless and derelict — survived until 1963. The building behind the Great Eastern 4-2-2 was No 2 shed dating from 1851; it had a 42ft central turntable serving 16 stalls. *Author's collection*

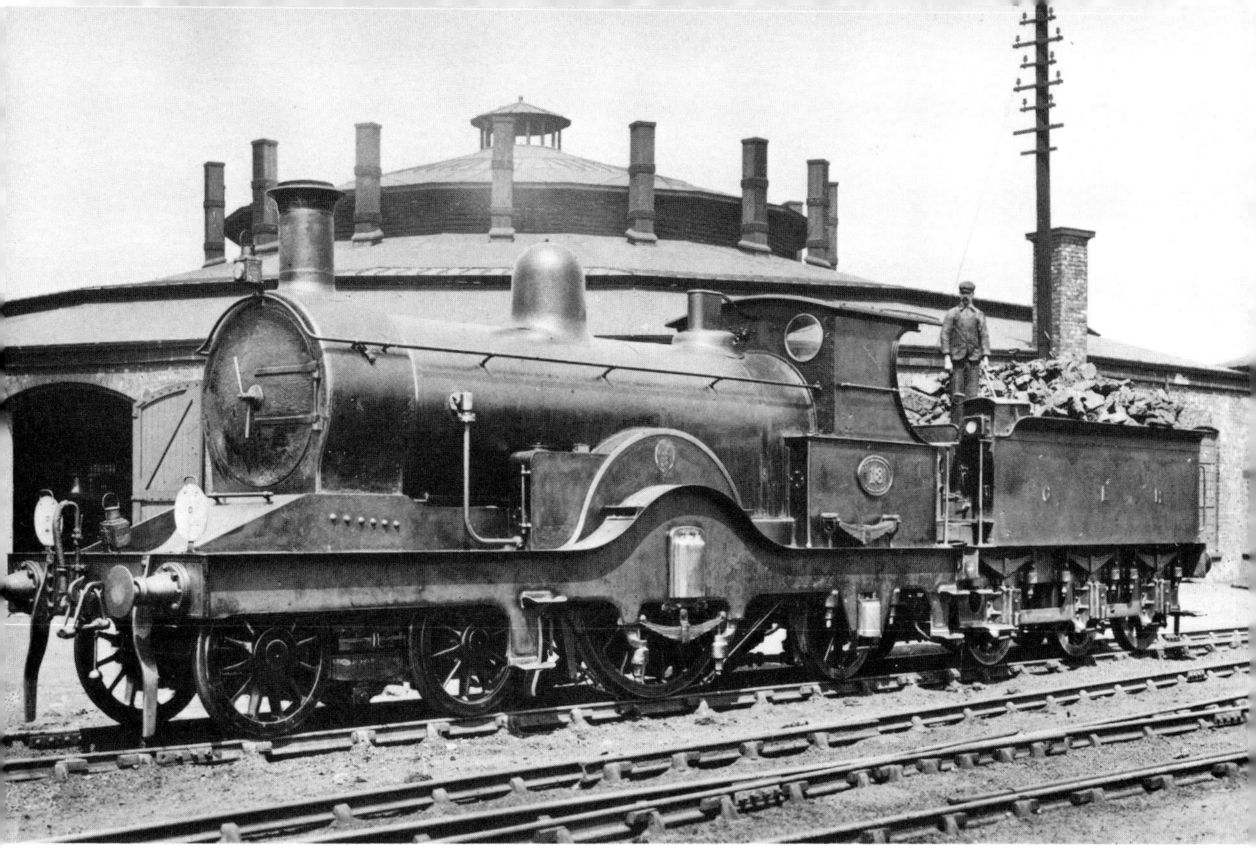

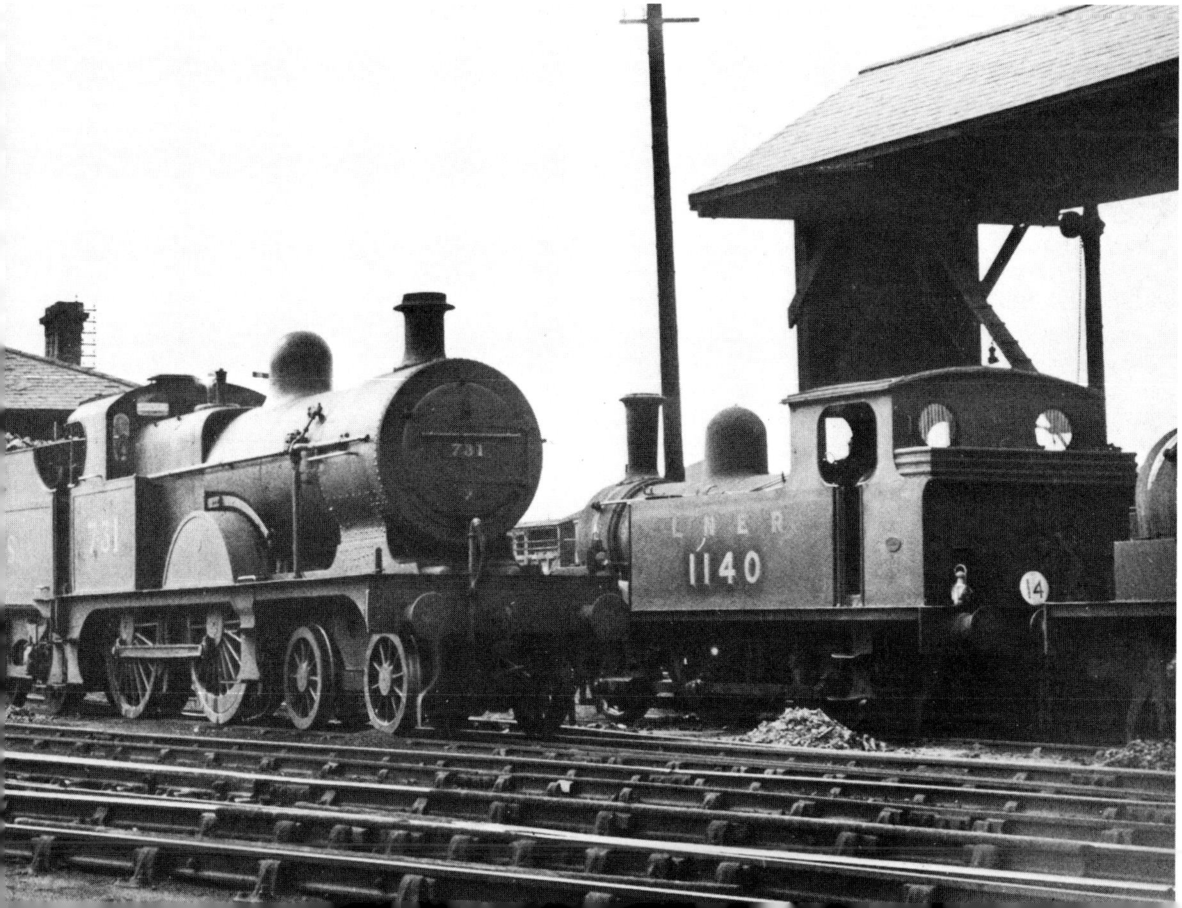
731
L N E R
1140
14

many of them compounds, with continuous splashers on the 2-4-0 and 4-4-0 engines, double-window cabs on all tender engines, and the clean, uncluttered lines on both tender and tank engines. There was also a great deal of standardisation.

Wilson Worsdell followed his brother in 1890 and brought even larger engines to the main line in the shape of the 'M1', 'R', 'R1' 4-4-0s, and the 'V' and '4CC' Atlantics. Goods workings were handled by the 'P1', 'P2' and 'P3' 0-6-0s and the 'T' and 'T1' 0-8-0s. There were also the 'S' and 'S1' 4-6-0s, some built specially for express goods working on the main line.

Local passenger services around York were handled by Class 901 and 1463 2-4-0 engines displaced from the main line by the 4-4-0s, which in turn were displaced by Atlantics. Tank engines were never common at York, which had few short distance services, although at times prior to 1914 the Class O 0-4-4T could occasionally be seen on Scarborough trains. The ubiquitous 'BTP' 0-4-4T engines worked some local services, and they could occasionally be seen as carriage pilots, although for many years the station pilot duties were performed by 'J71' 0-6-0T engines.

The appointment of Vincent Raven as Chief Mechanical Engineer in 1910 brought the famous Class Z Atlantics to the main line between York and Edinburgh, with their 15 years of superiority,

Above: No 3 shed was authorised in 1863 and it was used by the Midland engines from 1870. It had a 45ft turntable and 18 stalls and it is easily distinguishable because each stall had its own gabled section. Note the weather vane on the roof, with the 'Jenny Lind' 2-2-2 'cock'. The 4-4-0T *Holdsworth* was on its way from the Metropolitan Railway at Neasden to the Bradford Corporation Waterworks line at Pateley Bridge, perhaps better known as the Nidd Valley Light Railway. The date was 1907. *Author's collection*

Right: Even though the shed was literally falling down around them the 'J71' and 'J72' pilots continued to be housed in No 3 shed. Eventually it became unsafe to enter the building and the remains of the roof were removed, leaving the walls standing — and it still continued to be used by the pilots until demolished in 1963. *Real Photographs*

but his Pacific engines were turned down in favour of the Gresley Pacifics, which performed many years of good work, appearing at York from both former North Eastern and Great Northern sheds. As their capabilities were realised they became regular performers on Newcastle-King's Cross trains, cutting out much of the long-established engine changing at York. Gresley engines also appeared on fast goods and excursion work, notably the 'J39' 0-6-0s and the 'K3'

2-6-0s, but even so some of the NER engines, particularly the 'B16' 4-6-0s, outlasted the Gresley types. In fact York has never been the same without its 'B16s' and at one time all 69 of the class were stationed at York.

Also common at York were the 'D49' 4-4-0s — 'Shires' and 'Hunts' — which worked into York from surrounding sheds such as Scarborough, Hull and Leeds, with a number usually allocated to York shed. In the 1940s and 1950s the most common type was the 'V2' 2-6-2, which could be seen on branch and main line trains, passenger and goods, night and day!

In LNER days some local services were worked by petrol or steam (Sentinel) railcars but it was the introduction of British Railways' multiple-unit railcars that swept away all the engines formerly used on the local passenger trains. A few years later the same applied on the main line as diesel-electric locomotives appeared; those making the greatest impression were the noisy and speedy 'Deltics', which disappeared in December 1981, displaced by the glorified railcars known as High Speed Trains!

When in 1924 three further Raven Pacifics were built it was decided to name the first of these *City of York*, but this class was not perpetuated by the LNER and No 2402 was withdrawn on 25 July 1936 after covering 456,533 miles in just over 12 years' service. Although the engine spent most of its life working from Gateshead shed it spent its last two years working from York shed, to which it was transferred on 13 August 1934. The City gained further recognition in 1939, when on 4 April, 'V2' No 4818 was named *St Peter's School, York, AD627* by the School Captain. Another naming ceremony took place at York on 4 April 1963 when No D9002 was named *The King's Own Yorkshire Light Infantry* by the Colonel of the Regiment.

Engine Sheds
A plan of York dated 1870 shows six engine sheds serving the original station — three straight sheds and three roundhouses. One of the straight sheds was provided for the York & North Midland engines, and another for the Great North of England engines, both believed to be to the designs of G. T. Andrews and built in 1840. The architect's signed drawing of the GNE shed still exists in the Victoria & Albert Museum and shows that it could accommodate only six engines standing transversely, each stall reached by a turnplate on a line running through the shed on one side.

The turnplates could only accommodate the engine, and the tender had to be detached when the locomotive was stabled. In a report dated

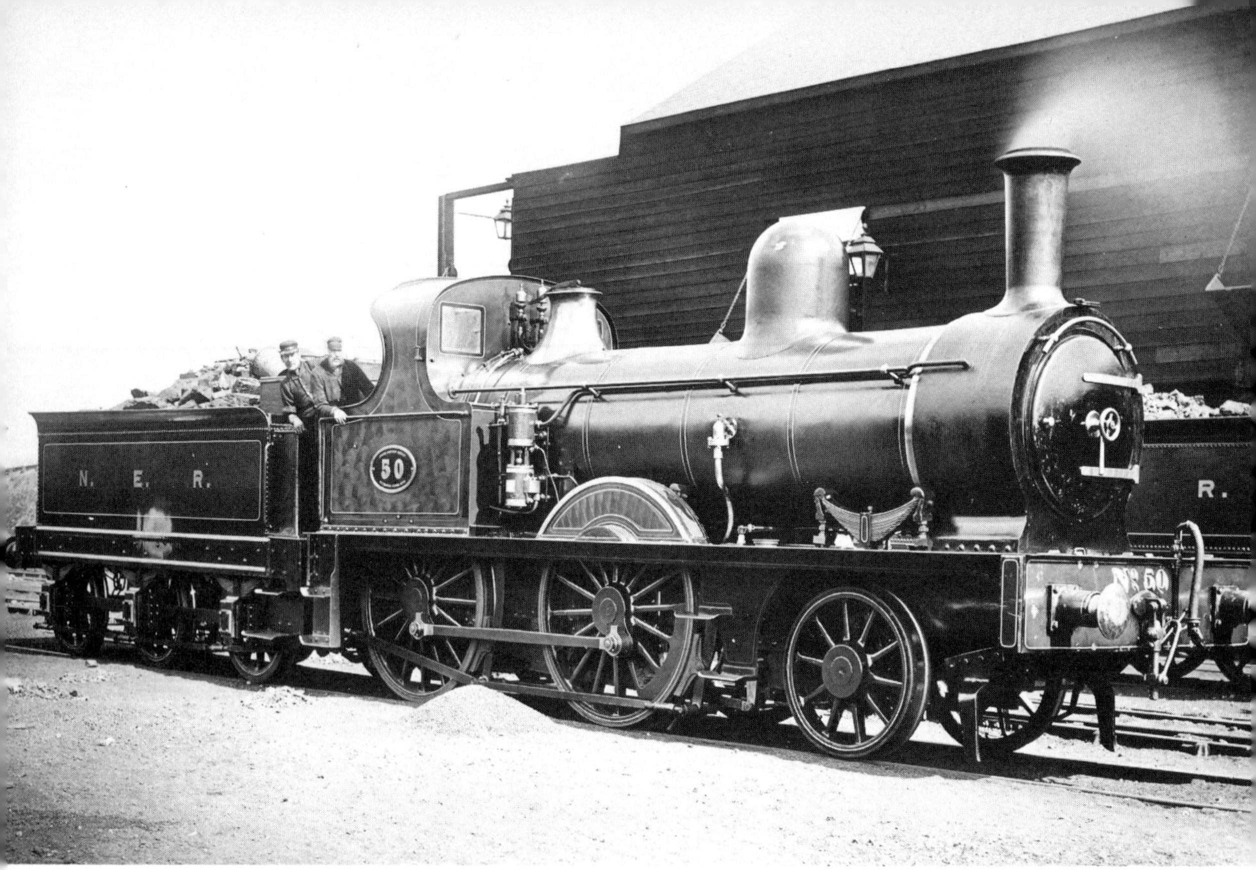
N. E. R.
50
No 60
R.

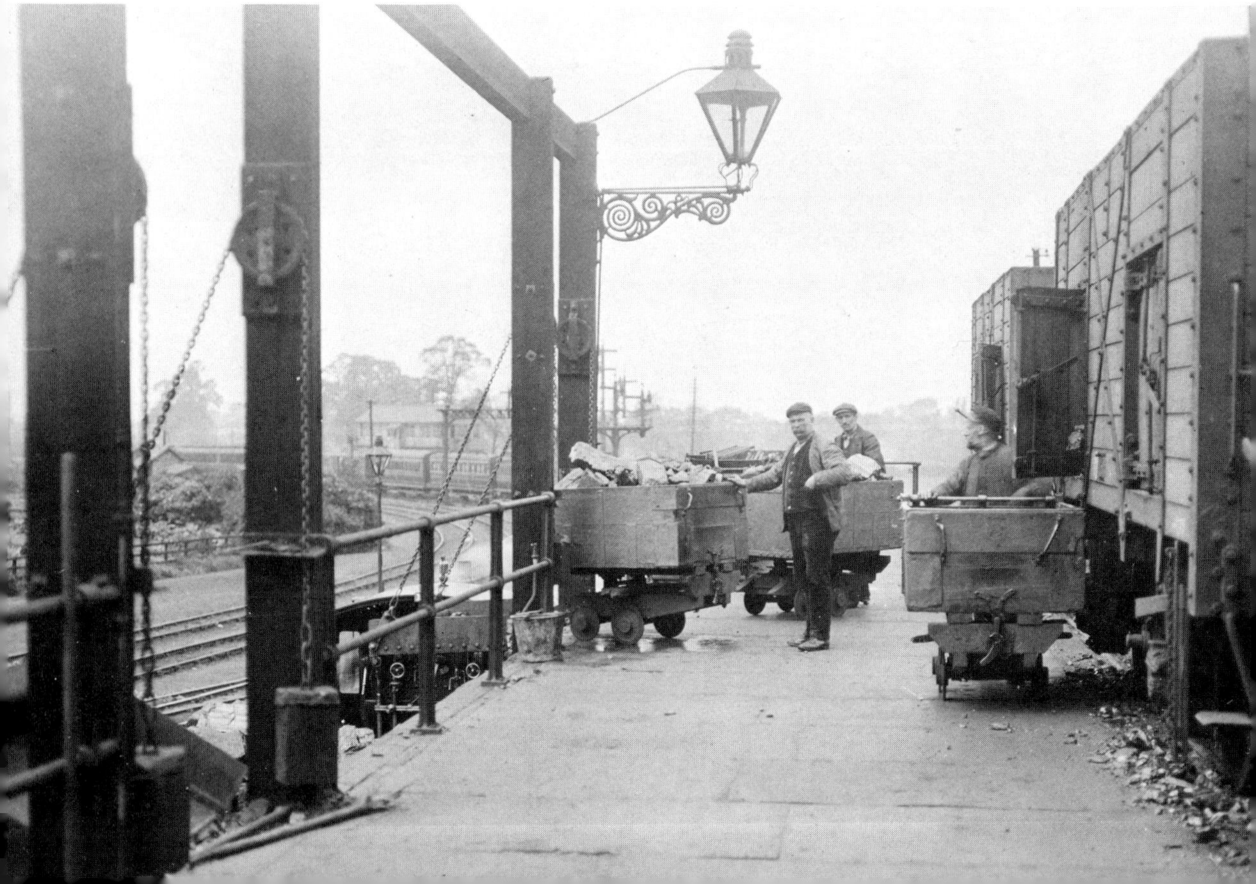

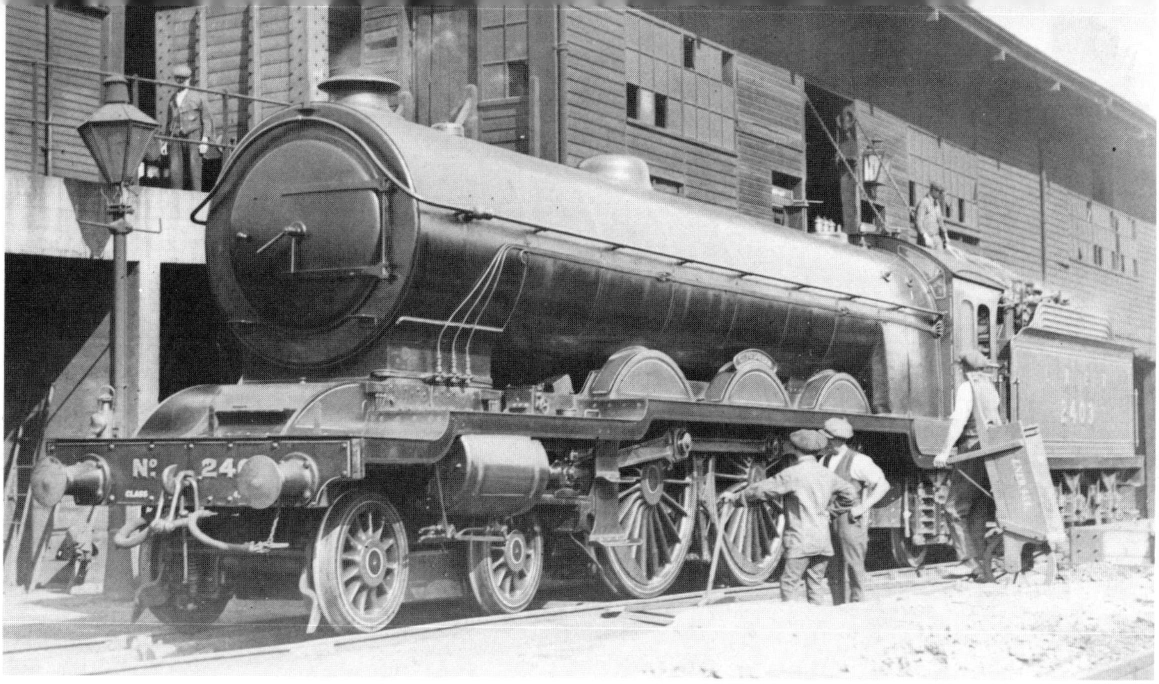

Above left : A new shed to hold 60 engines was authorised in 1875, to be built at the north end of the new station then under construction. When completed it consisted of three roundhouses under one roof, arranged in an L shape. In the yard to the north of the shed there was a coaling stage, with protection for the coalmen provided by a large wooden structure. No 19th century views of the shed itself are known, but the coal stage became a favourite background for some photographers, as this early view of 2-4-0 No 50 shows. It was photographed c1888. *LPC*

Left: After about 20 years the coal stage lost its roof and as it was not replaced the men had to work in the open. This is a view taken on top of the stage, with tubs of coal ready for tipping down the chutes on to the tenders. The engine standing awaiting coaling is a Lancashire & Yorkshire Atlantic. *Author's collection*

Above: When the fourth roundhouse was added in 1915 the original coal stage had to be replaced by a larger stage further north in the shed yard. This too had a wooden superstructure when new, but it was removed after the provision of a mechanical coaling plant in 1932, although the reinforced concrete ramp and stage remained for some years longer. The engine is Raven Pacific No 2403 *City of Durham. C. Ord*

Right: The Mitchell mechanical coaling plant commissioned in 1932, with four chutes fed from bunkers with a total capacity of 500 tons. It was demolished, with some difficulty, in 1970. *R. F. Dean*

Right: The reinforced concrete water tower holding 100,000 gallons was erected in 1909, and demolished by explosives in 1973. The NER was a pioneer in the use of reinforced concrete and used it for many large structures pre-1914. The engine in the shed yard is No 2404 *City of Ripon*, the Raven Pacific rebuilt with a Gresley boiler. *C. Ord*

Above: The 70ft Mundt non-balancing electric turntable was installed in 1932 and 27 years later was used by preserved Midland compound No 1000, which had worked in on a rail-tour. *Author*

Right: An interior view at the North shed in June 1935. The engines, from left to right, are: No 190 Class X3 2-2-4T; No 111 'K3' 2-6-0; No 2060 'J25' 0-6-0; No 1956 'J24' 0-6-0 and No 1821 'J24' 0-6-0. *L. Hanson*

5 January 1841 the design was criticised by Robert Stephenson and at some subsequent date the shed was changed to a normal three-road shed. The origin of the third straight shed is unknown, but it remained standing until the 1937/8 alterations, although not then in use for locomotive purposes. One of the two Andrews sheds was demolished to make way for the 1877 station, but the other, possibly the GNE shed, remained standing until 1963. As the importance of York increased, bringing in more trains and requiring more engine accommodation, two roundhouses were built in the 1850s, and another was authorised in 1863; these three sheds were situated in the triangle formed by the lines to north and south out of the 1841 station, and the North Junction to Holgate Junction curve. The first two sheds each had a 42ft turntable and 16 roads, and the later roundhouse had a 45ft turntable and 18 roads. The 1863 building was surmounted by a large weather vane, which used a 2-2-2 locomotive as the 'cock'.

In the re-arrangement of the tracks for the 1877 station the three roundhouses were unaffected and continued in use, together with the old GNE shed. With the opening of the Swinton & Knottingley Joint line in 1879 the Midland Railway requested accommodation for the engines working the Sheffield trains and initially space was allocated at the new shed north of the station which consisted of three roundhouses (with a fourth added in 1915), but a change of policy meant that the Midland engines were stabled in the 1863 roundhouse at the south end. The oldest 'foreigner' at York, the Great Northern, used the remaining straight shed adjacent to the three roundhouses.

The next move at the south end of the station was to convert the redundant Locomotive Works boiler shop into an engine shed for use by the 'foreign' engines visiting York, in conjunction with the opening of the new Locomotive Yard box in 1909. A 60ft turntable was provided at the same time to make the shed self-contained, and this later was used for transferring engines to and from the Queen Street Railway Museum; the turntable was installed at Southport's Steamport Railway Museum in 1981 and brought into use at Easter 1982.

As a result of the Grouping the LMS engines working into York were concentrated at the Queen Street shed, leaving the roundhouses on the opposite side of the line for North Eastern Area engines. After 10 years of this arrangement the LMS shed was closed in 1933 and the engines moved back to the old shed complex, taking over the straight shed from the GN Section engines, which then moved to the North shed.

One of the roundhouses was destroyed by fire in 1921 but the other two remained in use until 1961, although not demolished until 1963. After being vacated by the LMS engines in 1933 the Queen Street building was used for various purposes — it housed some of the surplus exhibits from the Railway Museum; it was used for stabling the various inspection saloons used by the officers at the Area headquarters, and it was also used as a clean environment for the first diesel-electric shunters to be stationed at York.

The increasing number of Pacific engines in the 1920s (when most main line engines were changed at York) caused delay as there was no suitable turntable and it was not until 1932 that a 70ft turntable was brought into use. This was electrically operated and of the Mundt non-balancing type supplied by Messrs Ransome & Rapier Ltd; at the same time a mechanical coaling plant was installed, supplied by Mitchell Conveyor & Transport Co Ltd at a cost of £8,073.

In 1934 the five Raven Pacifics were transferred to York but because of their length they could not be accommodated inside the shed, until in 1935 a 70ft turntable was authorised for No 4 shed (the 1915 building) and this was followed by the transfer to York of Gresley Pacific engines to replace the short-lived Raven engines as they were withdrawn in 1936/7.

Then on 29 April 1942 came the air-raid on York, when the shed suffered a direct hit, causing severe damage to 'B16' No 925 and 'A4' No 4469 *Sir Ralph Wedgwood* and bringing about their premature withdrawal. The shed was patched up and continued in use and in 1954 the 70ft turntable in No 4 shed was replaced by a new one by John Boyd & Co (Engineers) of Annan. In 1957/8 No 1 shed, still with a 45ft turntable, and No 2 shed, with a 50ft turntable, were demolished and replaced by a straight shed/repair shop, whilst No 3 and No 4 sheds were rebuilt, remaining as two round-houses under one roof and retaining their 60ft and 70ft turntables. They later formed the main hall of the National Railway Museum.

The last steam locomotives were transferred away on 25 June 1967 and in 1970 the coaling plant was demolished, followed in June 1973 by the demolition of the nearby ferro-concrete 100,000 gallon water tank.

At the turn of the century York shed had 148 engines and 585 men but in 1914, with more

Left: **Working on trials from York shed in the early 1930s was the Kitson-Still steam and diesel locomotive which Kitson & Co hoped would supersede the old fashioned steam locomotive. However, the rapid development in the 1930s of the diesel engine, with mechanical or electric transmission, with no need for a boiler, meant that Kitson's hopes were dashed. The engine was photographed at York in June 1932 when it was undergoing tests on York-Hull freight trains.**
W. H. Whitworth

Right: **York shed usually housed one of the four 2-2-4T engines kept in spotless condition for working officers' inspection saloons. No 1679 was photographed in No 1 shed at the North depot.** *Author's collection*

Left: **In BR days various types of engines were used on the saloon specials, such as 'B1' No 61319 in September 1964. However, the engine chosen did receive some attention from the cleaners! This saloon No E902177E (originally NER No 305) is now preserved. It was photographed leaving Platform 7 for the Scarborough branch.** *Author*

Right: The scene at York shed after the German bombing in April 1942. The damaged 'B16', No 925, can be seen above and to the right of the chimney of the '04' in the foreground. *BR*

Left: York shed yard from the top of the coaling plant on a Sunday afternoon on the occasion of a Lodging Turn strike in May 1949. *Author's collection*

Right: Roundhouses 1 and 2 at the north shed were demolished in 1957/8 and replaced by a straight shed and repair shop, with Nos 3 and 4 sheds being rebuilt into their present form, but now housing the National Railway Museum. Standing in the shed in steam days were Nos 60155 *Borderer*, 'K1' 62065 and 'WD' 90517. *E. Sanderson*

powerful engines and shorter hours, there were 116 engines and 722 men.

In 1925 the Great Northern engines stationed at York were transferred to North Eastern Area stock and subsequently used with the 'native' engines. The engines concerned were 'D2' 4-4-0 Nos 4180, 4386, 4387, 4396, 4398, and 'D3' No 4348, 'C1' 4-4-2 Nos 4424 and 4447, and 'C2' Nos 3984 and 3986; the two large Atlantics remained at York until 1943 when they were transferred to the Southern Area. During World War 2 Southern Railway 'King Arthur' 4-6-0s worked in from Heaton, and two ex-LBSCR 4-4-0s, SR Nos 2051 and 2068, were actually stationed at York. No USA 2-8-0 engines were stationed at York but they worked in from Heaton and Neville Hill, each of which had 25 of these engines.

Following the war came the flood of new 'B1' 4-6-0 engines, and the new Pacifics designed by Peppercorn and Thompson, with Nos 60121/38/53, and Nos 60522/4/6 actually stationed at York, but the Gresley 'A3' and 'A4' engines, together with the ever-present 'V2' engines, were the mainstay of the passenger traffic.

At first Nationalisation did not make a great deal of difference, but 4-6-0s Nos 73162-71 were received in 1957 and some '9F' 2-10-0s followed for heavy goods work. The greatest change was in the shunting work where 350hp diesel-electric shunters took over the yard work, although for a time the pilot engines serving the station remained steam. The first main line diesels were the English Electric Type 4 and at one time 30 were stationed

at York for all types of duties. The running shed remained in use for diesel locomotives but its importance decreased with the closure of branches and the use of DMU and HST sets, leading to its closure in January 1982, when all 37 main line locomotives were transferred away, leaving only a handful of shunters.

For many years York shed's top link steam turns were straightforward workings to Newcastle and back, some turns involving working a passenger train in one direction and a braked goods in the other. Most of York's local workings were to Harrogate, Hull, Leeds, Normanton, Pickering, Scarborough and Whitby, and engines reached York from such sheds as Darlington, Doncaster Gateshead, Heaton, Hull, Leeds, Normanton, Pickering, Saltburn, Scarborough, Selby and Whitby. After World War 1 York men's activities were extended to Grantham and Peterborough, reaching King's Cross only on excursions and with a conductor or pilot drvier. Eventually lodging turns to King's Cross were introduced, but in World War 2 these were abolished and when attempts were made to reintroduce them after the war the crews at York went on strike. However, the 'Deltic' locomotives, and accelerated timings meant that a York crew could work to London and back in a shift, the distance of 376 miles qualifying them for a worthwhile mileage payment.

Since the reintroduction of steam specials York crews have played a large part in working the many locomotives which have worked in the area, and there is close co-operation between the

Above left: Inside the repair shop in May 1965 was 'J27' No 65823, one of the engines built for the North Eastern by the North British Locomotive Company of Glasgow. *N. E. W. Skinner*

Above: Like most large depots York shed had a steam crane to handle derailments etc. A new crane supplied in 1912 came from Craven Bros of Manchester and had a capacity of 35 tons. *BR*

Centre right: Adjoining the running shed in Leeman Road was the oil gas works, making gas for illuminating coaches. An underground gas main supplied hydrants in York station and the oil gas was distributed to outstations such as Harrogate and Scarborough by gas tank wagons. *Author's collection*

Right: The Civil Engineer's Yard, also in Leeman Road, had its own locomotive shed, built to house 'Y1' Sentinel No 45. The 1877 main line to the north can be seen in the background as it curves round to join the original route at York Yard North. *N. E. W. Skinner*

Right: Sentinel shunter No 45, a Departmental engine specifically purchased by the LNER for shunting the District Engineer's yard at York. *BR*

Left: The District Engineer was also provided with road transport to carry men to locations where work was in hand, such as this ex-Maidstone & District Leyland Tiger FKO 73 (BR ELB 0106). *N. E. W. Skinner*

York Locomotive Works

Below left: A view of the Locomotive Works from the City Walls, with Nos 1 and 2 erecting shops on the right. The old York & North Midland shops are in the left background, with the Railway Institute on the extreme left. The photograph was taken about 1900. *Author's collection*

Above right: Interior of the Boiler Shop. This building became an engine shed in 1909 and until 1932 was used by the LMS engines stationed at York. *Author's collection*

Right: The Machine Shop, which later became the main hall of the Queen Street Railway Museum. *Author's collection*

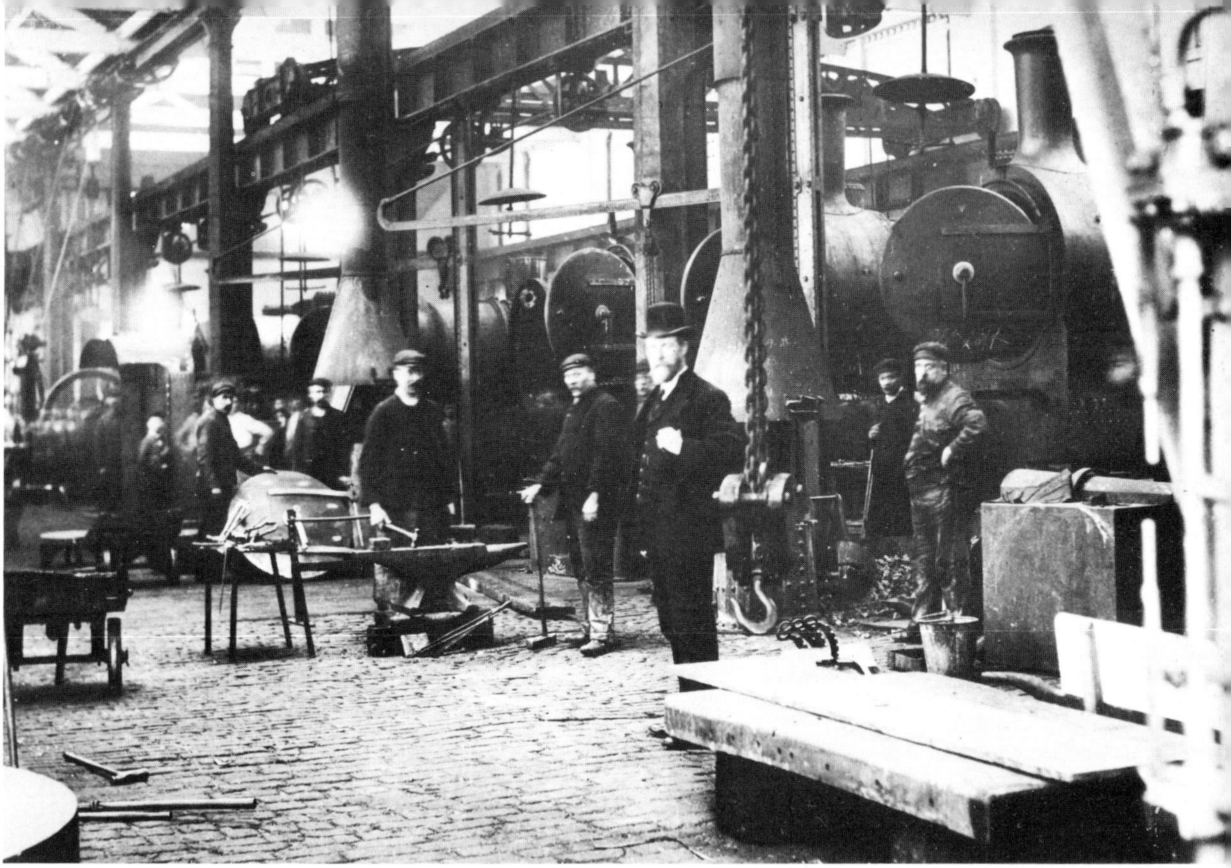

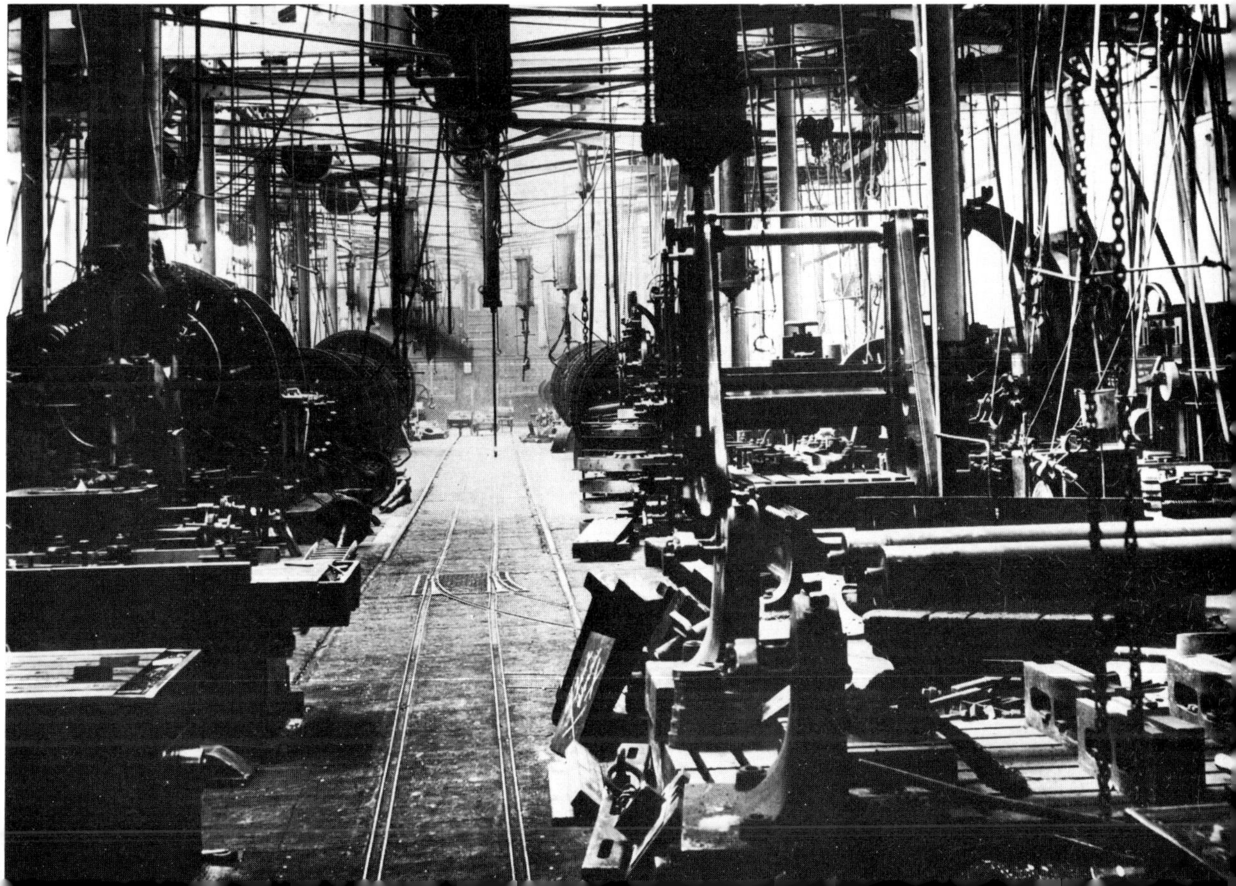

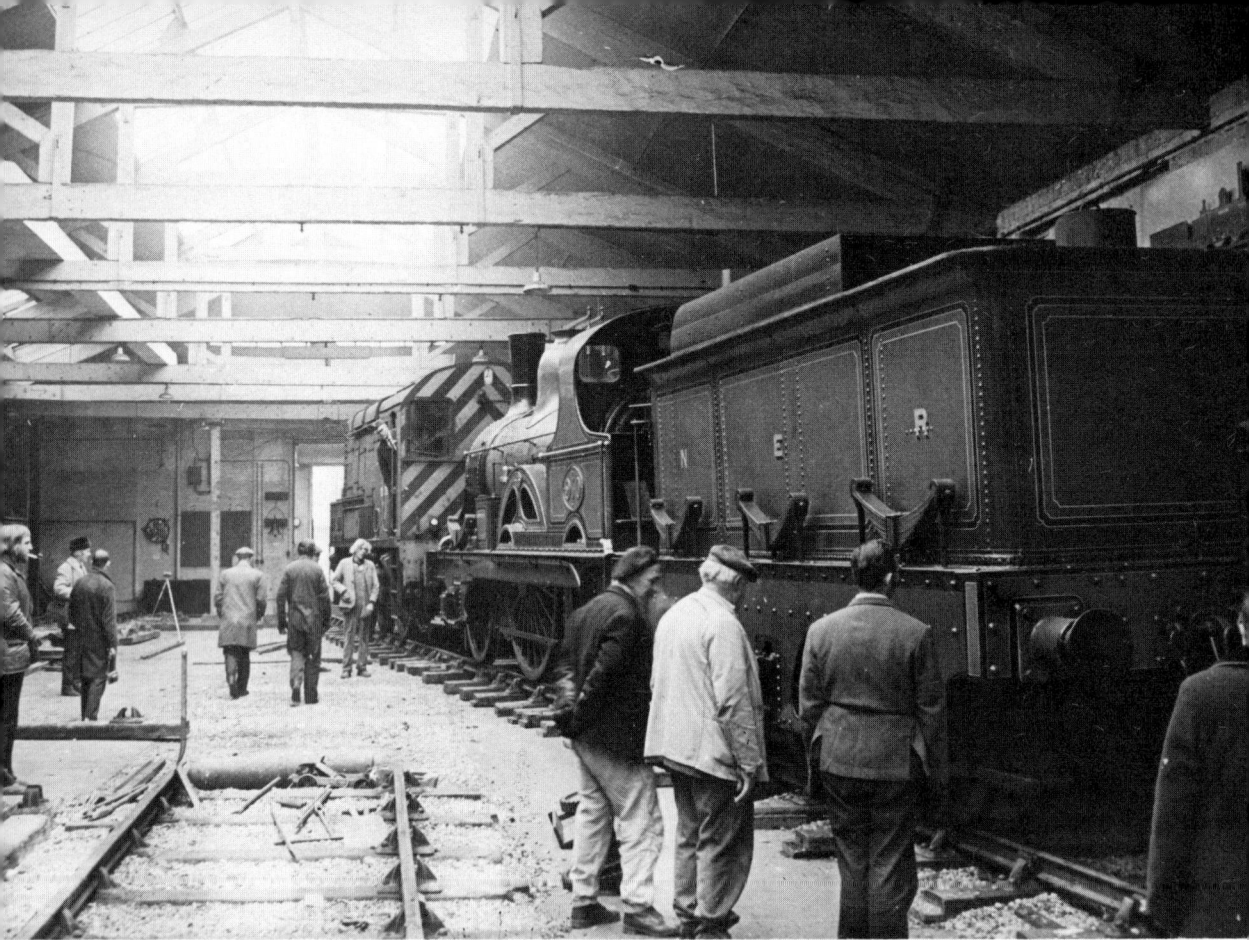

shed staff and the National Railway Museum which, of course, is housed in the former steam motive power depot.

Above: **The demise of Queen Street Museum in 1974, with NER No 910 being hauled out on temporary track.** *Author's collection*

Right: **The interior of No 1 Erecting Shop with engines undergoing repair c1900.** *Author's collection*

Locomotive Works, Carriage Works and Wagon Works

In March 1842 the York & North Midland Railway invited tenders for the construction of workshops at York, and in October 1844 further tenders were invited for additional workshops, and engine houses. These were required to maintain the company's rapidly growing fleet of locomotives and rolling stock, and the site chosen was outside the City Walls, adjacent to where the temporary station had been built in 1839. By 1865 the area was occupied by three Fitting Shops, two Smiths' Shops, and a Joiners' Shop in one block, with a separate Wagon Shop. These were all situated on the west side of the line from the Tanner Row station to the south, with six engine houses on the opposite side of the line.

When the Works was built the Y&NM was purchasing all its locomotives from contractors and thus they were used only for maintenance

purposes. Even in NER days very few engines were actually built at York, although Class 398 0-6-0s Nos 52, 134 and 266, and 'BTP' 0-4-4Ts Nos 290 and 305 were turned out in 1884. Between 1899 and 1904 40 'BTP' engines were rebuilt at York as 0-6-0T engines and reclassified '290'; 27 became BR property and No 1438, built by Hawthorn & Co in 1875 and rebuilt at York in 1904, ran until February 1961 and, as No 68408, was the last 'J77' engine in service.

When the Wagon Shop became redundant in 1867 it was replaced by a locomotive erecting shop, and a similar shop was later built alongside. However, the accommodation at York was cramped and there was no room for expansion; in addition the NER was in dispute with the local authority regarding the rates and as a large new erecting shop had been completed at Darlington in 1903 it was decided to close the York Works and transfer the work to Darlington. This took effect in 1905 and over the years the buildings were adapted for other uses; for instance in 1907 some of the buildings were taken over by the expanding Road Motor Department, and later No 1 Erecting Shop was converted to a Carriage Shed, although subsequently used for 'Unclaimed Goods'. On 10 February 1926 No 2 Erecting Shop was formally opened as a gynasium in connection with the nearby Railway Institute.

In the 1920s the two fitting/machine shops in the Y&NM part of the old Works were used to house exhibits being collected together as the nucleus of the LNER Railway Museum, which opened in 1928: before that date the items were only available for inspection by prior appointment. Although the Museum concentrated on items from the old NER it did accept relics from other sections of the LNER and from the three other main line companies, so that *City of Truro* from the Great Western, *Columbine* from the London & North Western, and *Gladstone* from the London, Brighton & South Coast could be seen alongside the North Eastern's *Aerolite* and the Great Northern's *Henry Oakley*. The Museum closed its doors on 31 December 1973 to allow

time to prepare the exhibits for their new home in the National Railway Musem. Later the surplus items were transferred to the Peter Allen Building at Leeman Road (the former Goods Warehouse) and demolition of the Museum buildings commenced on 5 April 1979. The site is now a car park.

By the 1860s the Wagon Shop at Queen Street had become too small and in 1867 it was decided that a Wagon Works should be established on the north side of what was then the Scarborough branch, near to North Junction. For many years wagons and vans were built at York, but in LNER days wagon construction was centred on Faverdale (Darlington) and Shildon, and York's main task was repair and overhaul work. In BR days some 400 wagons were dealt with each week, and in addition repairs were undertaken to containers, coaching vehicles (horse-boxes, carriage trucks etc), station equipment, and road vehicles. The Works covered an area of some 17 acres, of which $4\frac{1}{2}$ acres were roofed buildings.

On 9 September 1880 tenders were accepted for the erection of a Carriage Building Shop and a Paint shop at York, to be on the west side of the former main line to the north near North Junction. A further Carriage Shop was authorised in 1882 and extensions were carried out in 1883, so that in 1884 York Carriage Works was able to take

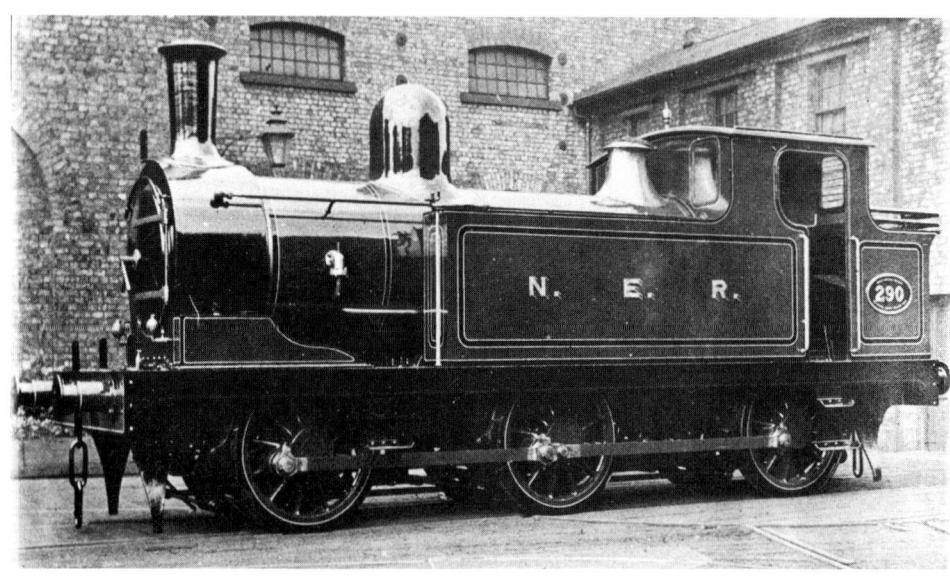

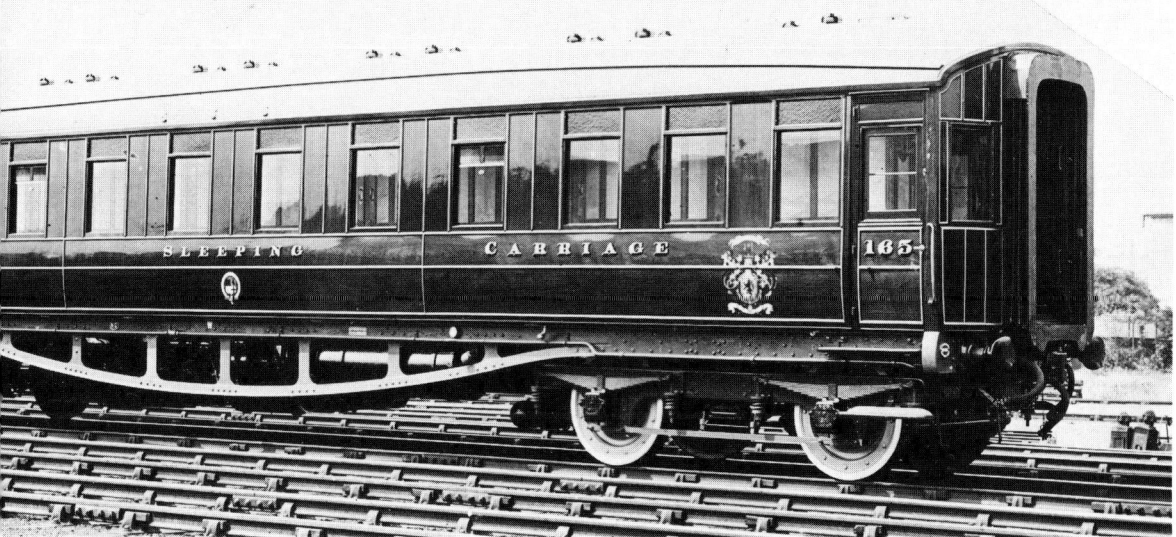

Top left: **Class BTP 0-4-4T No 290, one of the few engines built at York Works. It is the McDonnell version of the Fletcher 'BTP' engines and is one of a pair built in 1884.** *Author's collection*

Centre left: **In 1898 'BTP' No 290 entered York Works and in the following year emerged as a Class 290 0-6-0T! This was because the appearance of 70 Worsdell Class O 0-4-4T engines had rendered redundant many of the 'BTP' engines and between 1899 and 1904 40 were rebuilt to Class 290 at York. Both Nos 290 and 305 (the other York built 'BTP') retained their distinctive cabs until scrapped in BR days. The photograph was taken outside the Boiler Shop at York.** *Author's collection*

York Carriage Works

Left: **A change to elliptical roofs was made in 1906 but this first class Family Saloon was one of a pair built in 1911 and photographed in the yard of the Old Station when new. It ran until condemned in 1944.** *BR*

Top: **The North Eastern was well known for its Bain clerestory coaches, such as this Brake Third built at York in 1896.** *BR*

Above: **From 1895 York Carriage Works built vehicles for the East Coast Joint Stock fleet, such as this 56ft 6in 10-berth sleeping car, turned out in 1906 and condemned in 1931. The fish-bellied underframe was favoured by the NER but it was replaced by a normal frame in the 1920s.** *L. Ward collection*

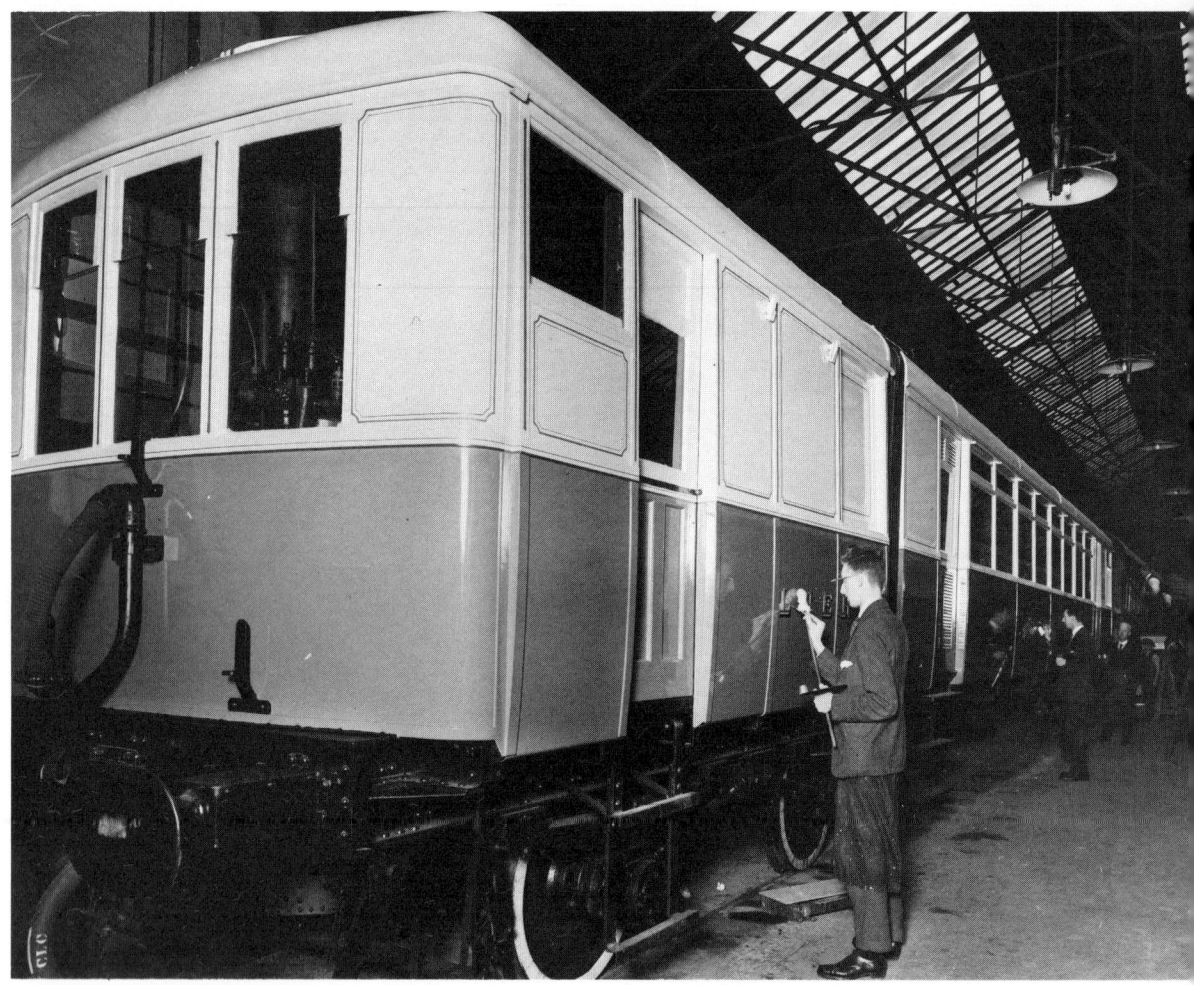

on the task of building and maintaining the whole of the NER's fleet of coaches.

At first all the coaches built at York ran on four or six wheels and the first bogie coach — a saloon for the Directors — was not built until 1891; even so bogie stock did not go into regular production until 1895. Also in 1895 York Works began to build vehicles for the East Coast Joint Stock fleet, previously the preserve of the Great Northern Railway, and in 1904 started to produce motor coaches and trailers for the North Tyneside electrified system. The NER clerestory roofed bogie coaches were designed by David Bain, but in 1902 he resigned from the North Eastern and moved to the Midland, where he became Carriage & Wagon Superintendent from 1 January 1903. The clerestory roof was abandoned in 1906, and in 1908 vestibule corridor stock was built at York for the company's more important services such as Leeds-Glasgow and Newcastle-Liverpool, mostly on two four-wheel bogies, but some magnificent

Above: **In LNER days the Carriage Works carried out the final painting, lining out, numbering and naming of the steam railcars purchased from Sentinel Waggon Works Ltd of Shrewsbury. This is No 29** *Rockingham* **receiving attention when new in 1928.** *BR*

Right: **British Railways Carriage and Wagon Works, York.**

dining cars were built, 65ft 6in over headstocks and carried on two six-wheel bogies. The Carriage Works also produced the bodies for the NER's pre-1914 fleet of motor buses and char-a-bancs.

After Grouping York turned its hand to the new coaches designed by H. N. Gresley from the Great Northern; these were intended for all Areas of the LNER, with the interiors arranged to suit particular traffic requirements. At the same time the whole of the North Eastern Area's carriage stock was maintained at York.

The old Carriage Building Shop was destroyed by fire in 1944 and the replacement buildings were specially designed and equipped for the progressive method of construction. Thus when British Railway was formed in 1948 the York complex was able to take on the task of building coaches to the new designs, and since then has continued to do so, producing locomotive hauled and electric multiple-unit stock for home and overseas.

A fine example of the work of York Carriage Works can be seen in the National Railway Museum, where the NER dynamometer car is on display. This was one of the last clerestory roof vehicles to be built in 1906 and it remained in use until BR days. Another surviving York vehicle is one of the pair of Royal saloons built for the East Coast route in 1908 — one at York for Queen Alexandra and the other at Doncaster for King Edward VII. Unfortunately it is the Doncaster built vehicle that is on display at York whilst the York built saloon is hidden away at Bressingham. What a pity the NRM authorities did not pay a tribute to the craftsmen of York by having the York vehicle on display in its home town. A less glamorous York vehicle — a North Eastern autocar (push-and-pull) coach — can be seen on the North York Moors Railway, purchased and restored by the North Eastern Railway Coach Group.

The North Eastern Railway was not the only concern which built steam locomotives for hauling passengers. There were some fine model locomotive engineers in York, but the most notable was Harry Clarkson, who founded the firm bearing his name, from which he retired in 1978. In addition to constructing numerous working and 'glass case' models he built the 2-8-2 *River Mite* for the Ravenglass & Eskdale Railway. This included parts from the steam tender which originally ran behind *River Esk* built for the Ravenglass line in 1927 by the Yorkshire Engine Co of Sheffield. *River Mite* was delivered to Ravenglass in December 1966 and was formally commissioned by working a special train on 20 May 1967. The engine has two outside cylinders 6in diameter by 8in stroke, and a working pressure of 165lb/sq in.

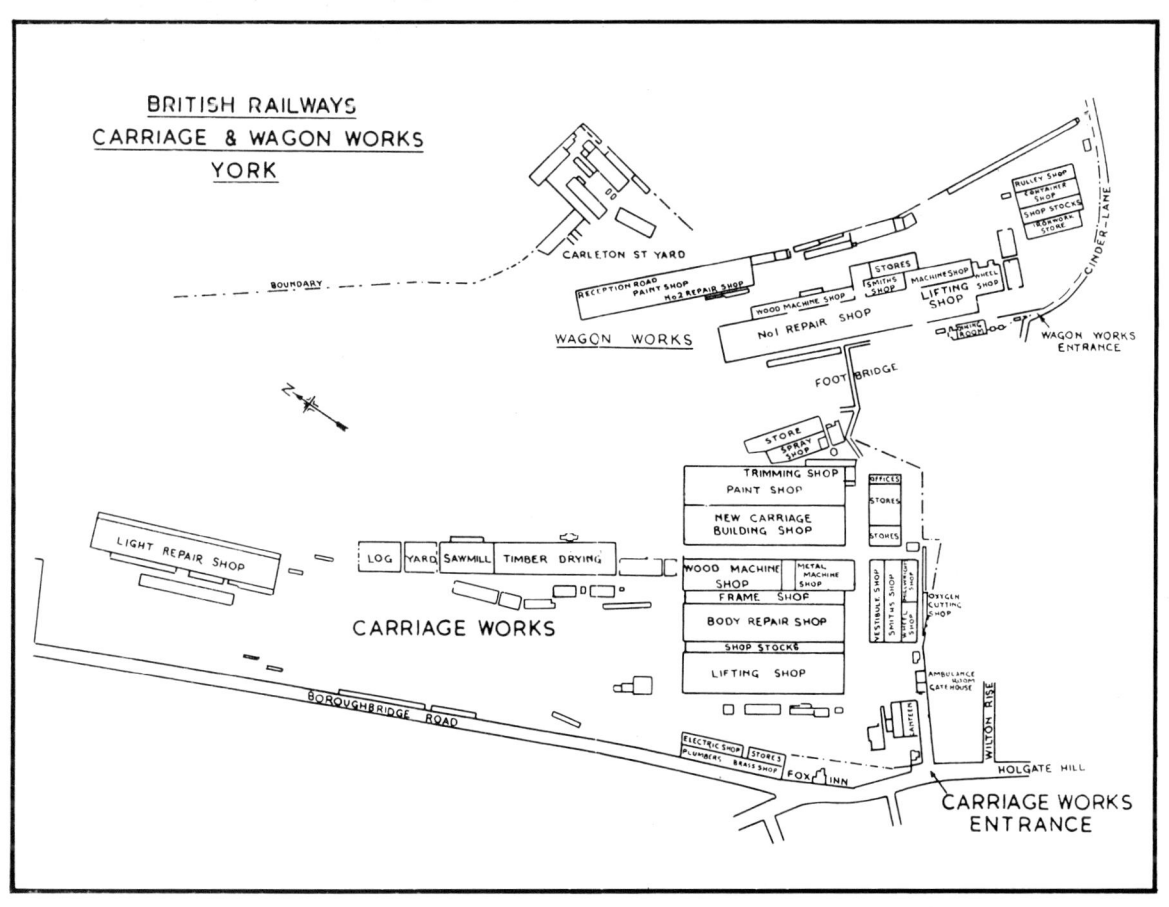

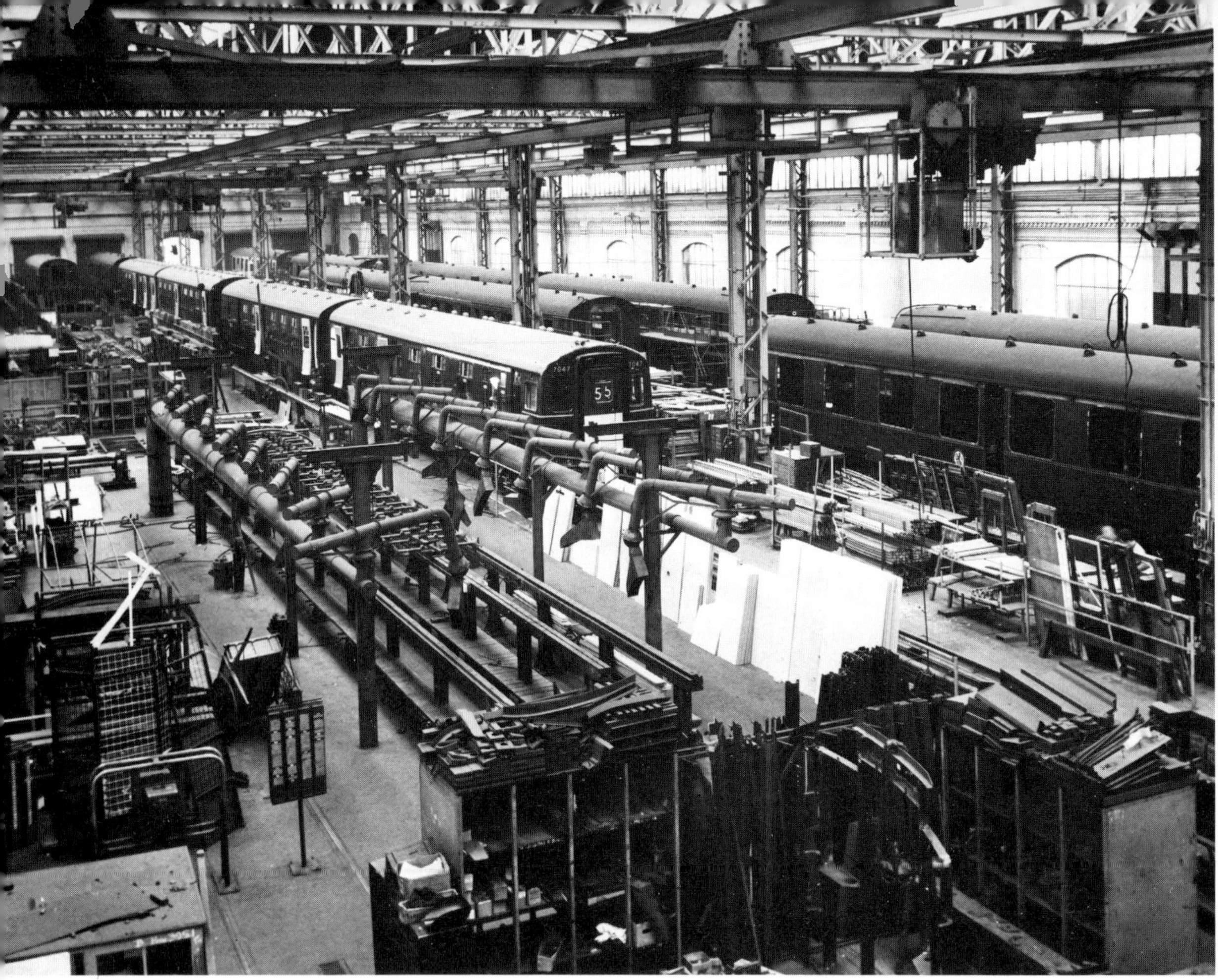
55

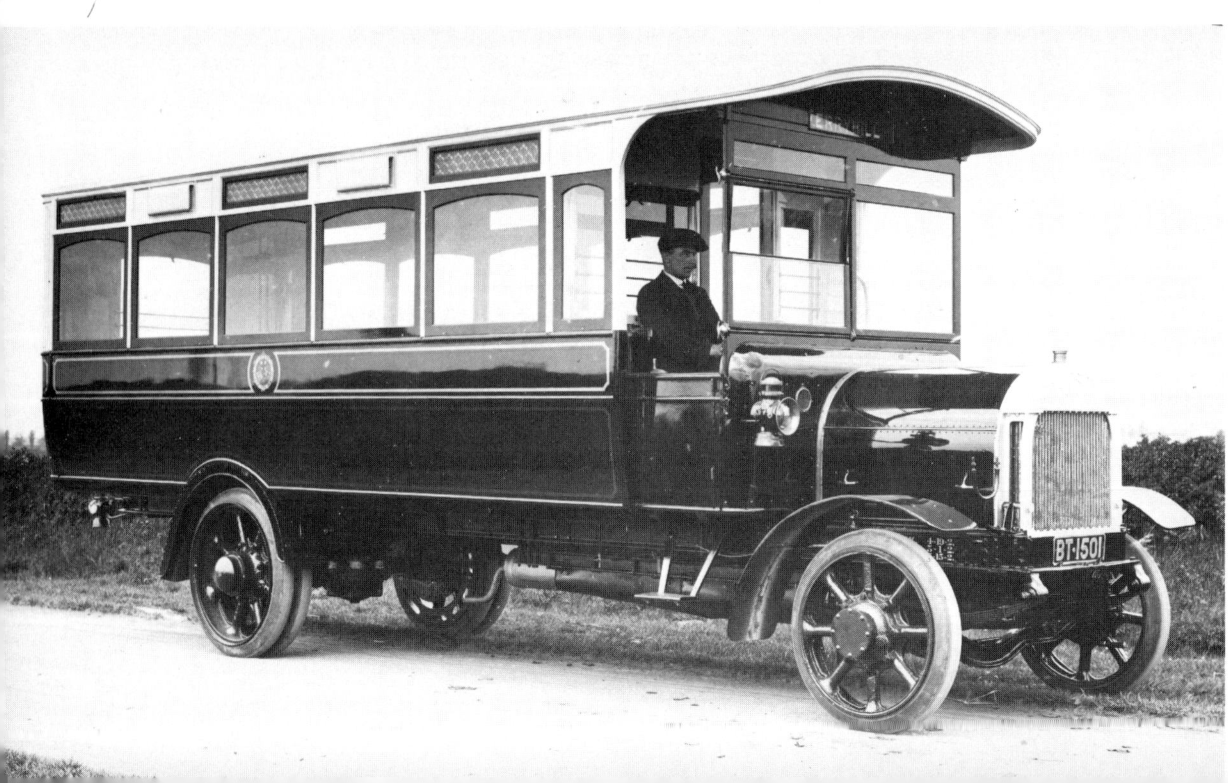
BT·1501

Left: Interior of York Carriage Works erecting shop in 1966, with electric stock for the Southern Region in the centre (4BIG No 7047). *BR*

Below left: Until 1914 the Carriage Works built the bodies for the NER's fleet of road vehicles, such as this Maudslay of 1914. However, a few weeks later the chassis was commandeered by the War Department and hurriedly fitted with a lorry body, but the bus bodies were stored by the NER and used after the war on new Leyland chassis. *BR*

Below: In its heyday the Wagon Works turned out vehicles like this 15 ton Road Van based at Marsh Lane. These vans were designed to carry small consignments of goods to wayside stations served by the branch pick-up goods trains — or Road Goods as they were known in the early days of railways. *BR*

Bottom: The Wagon Works, now closed, carried out repairs to LNER and BR vehicles. *BR*

Stations and Other Buildings

The York & North Midland Railway opened in 1839 with a temporary station outside the city walls, and it was 1841 before the permanent station was ready for use. In 1852 the Great Northern Railway, which had only recently started working into York, complained about the inadequacy of the station but it was not until the early 1860s that steps were taken to provide a new station, leading eventually to the NER (Yorkshire Lines) Bill submitted to Parliament in 1865. A figure of £200,000 was mentioned as the estimated cost! The Act received the Royal Assent on 23 July 1866, authorising a station between the York-Scarborough line and Thief Lane, together with two connecting lines, one 1¼ miles long forming the new main line through the station, and the other, one furlong in length, to connect the new main line to the existing Scarborough branch. The Act also empowered the NER to make a new road from the 1841 station to Thief Lane to give better access to the new station, and this involved breaching the City Walls adjacent to where the NER War Memorial now stands.

Preliminary work was, however, brought to a stand in 1867 when a disgruntled and determined shareholder asked some embarrassing questions about the company's accounts; although his accusations were proved to be unfounded they did bring about a lack of confidence in the NER, causing the shares to be depressed, and it was considered prudent to postpone the York station works.

In 1871 it was decided to have another look at the scheme and on 9 February 1872 tenders were considered, but no firm decision was reached; instead it was decided to appoint a special committee of Directors to supervise the York project. The estimated cost was now quoted as £189,420. The powers had to be extended in 1871 as the five years allowed for completion by the original Act were about to expire.

The new through station had to be built to serve the existing routes to north and south, together with the Scarborough branch, and to accomplish this it was sited north of Holgate Bridge so that trains from the south could run direct into the station. From the north end of the station a new line was built in the form of a letter 'S', joining the original route of 1841 at what is now York Yard North: However, there is no trace of an actual junction at this point and the new and old passenger lines did not connect until Skelton Junction (formerly Poppleton Junction) was reached. The old main line from the north continued in use as York Goods Yard, with sidings serving the Carriage Works, Wagon Works and Goods Station, and eventually also the Engineer's Yard.

The only section of line that had to be removed was that from York Yard South (formerly North Junction) into the Old Station, which ran across the site of the new station, but the course of the 1841 line could easily be discerned until the 1930s by the position of a one-time engine shed which, from 1877, was at an acute angle to the

Above right: **A great drawback to the smooth working of the 1841 station was that it was a terminus. In 1877 a fine new through station was opened, with 13 platforms, all bays except two. Built on a sweeping curve to fit in with the existing tracks the result was a most impressive station which is still in use today — and looks like being in use for many years to come.**

Access between the two sides of the station was by a subway. The Platform signalbox can be seen to the left of the clock, and the present footbridge is in line with the centre of the box. Note the painted decoration on the columns, and the cast decoration at the top. The colour scheme was maroon, pale mauve and white. The illumination was by gas.
Crown Copyright, National Railway Museum, York

Right: **Looking north along the main platform in 1907. The footbridge was added in 1900 to supplement the subway. Lighting is still by gas, although some arc lamps have made their appearance with the opening of the company's own power station.** *Author's collection*

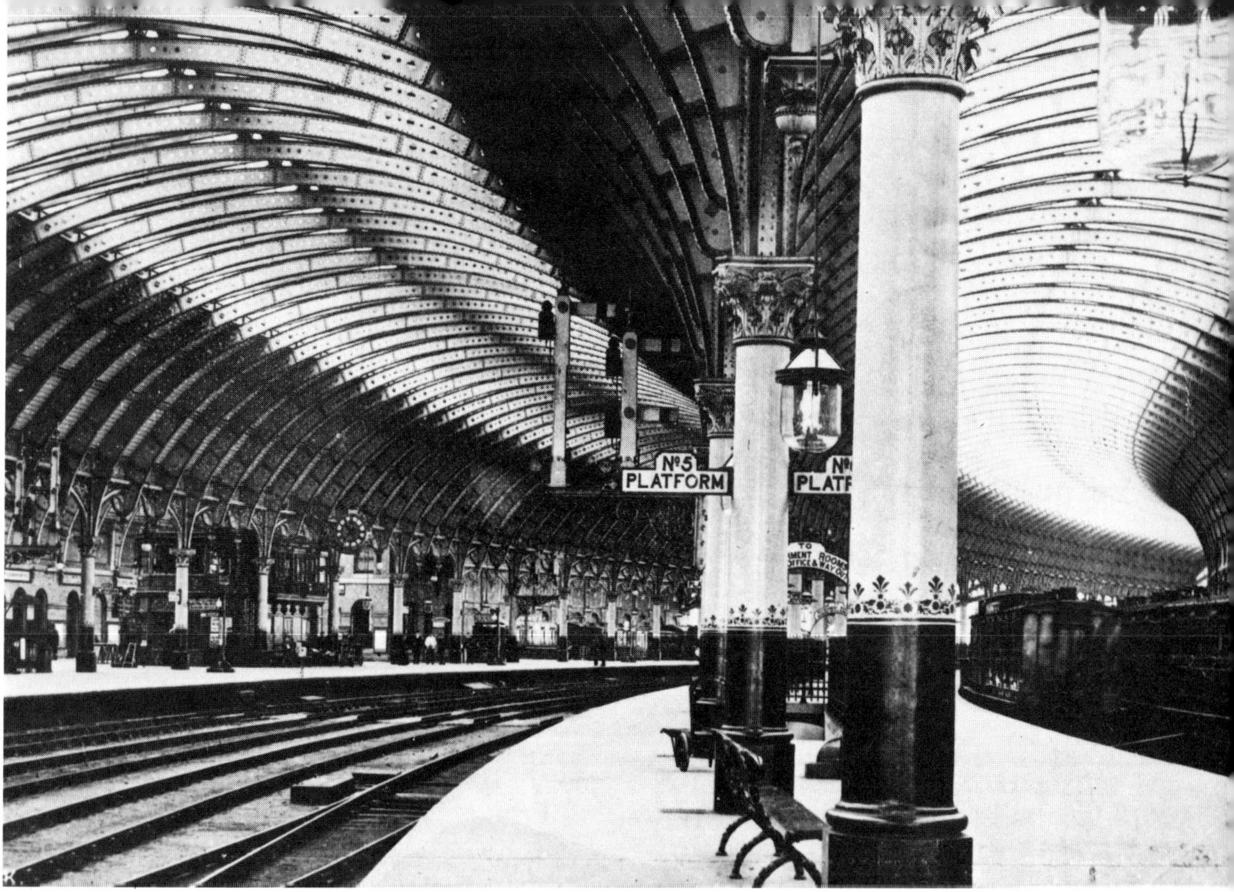
Nº5
PLATFORM

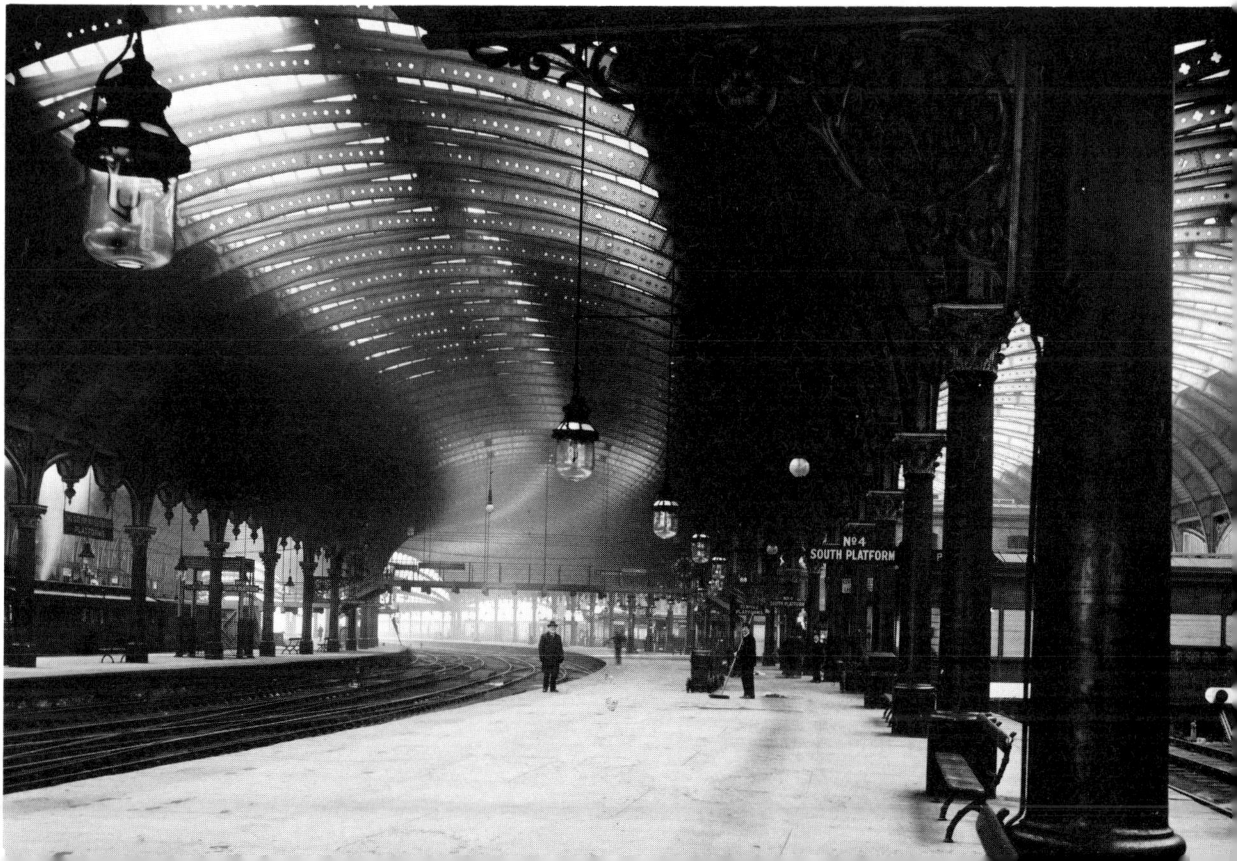
Nº4
SOUTH PLATFORM

new running lines. This building was demolished to make way for Platforms 15 and 16.

At the north end of the new station the former Scarborough line from North Junction crossed the new main line on the level, but before it reached Scarborough Bridge it was joined by the lines from the various platforms used by Scarborough bound trains — 4, 5, 6, 7, 8, 9 and later 14. The section of line from these connections to York Yard South became a goods only line from 1877. In the 1930s alterations, Platforms 15 and 16 were also given access to the Scarborough branch but in 1968 the crossing over the main line was removed for three months for repairs, leading to the temporary withdrawal of Scarborough line facilities from Platforms 14, 15 and 16. Down trains using Platform 14 had to stop at the footbridge so that they could be routed to the north or to the east, and to allow this the north end of the platform had to curve round to suit Scarborough bound trains. The final removal of the Scarborough line connections in 1975 meant that Platform 14 could be extended and the north end realigned to suit its use by main line trains only. This meant that down main line trains could draw up to the end of the platform instead of stopping short as they had done since 1938.

Above: **Looking south from No 4 platform c1907, with the old Locomotive Yard signalbox (replaced 1909) in the distance. Note the one-time engine shed on the extreme right is at an angle to the 1877 lines of the new station. When this shed was built it was parallel to the lines leading from North Junction to the Old Station — a route which had to be abandoned with the building of the 1877 station.** *LPC*

Right: **This view has been published on a number of occasions over the last 75 years, but not once has it been pointed out that what we now know as the Up Main ended in buffer stops just out of the picture. The Down Doncaster line and its connections were designed for the period when the down East Coast trains used No 4 platform so as to be conveniently placed for the Refreshment Rooms.**

In a painting of this scene, now in the National Railway Museum, the painter has altered the indication of some of the signals on the gantry at the end of No 4 platform, so that they give an indication which was impossible and which, in any case, would lead any up train on to the Down Doncaster line!

The signalbox on the left is the old Locomotive Yard box and the engine shed mentioned in the previous illustration is behind the box, with a large ventilator on the roof. To the left of the box is No 1 roundhouse, destroyed by fire in 1921. Locomotive Works on extreme right. *LPC*

To carry the Scarborough branch across the River Ouse a cast iron bridge with two 75ft spans was built, with the centre pier supported on 28 cast iron piles 24ft long driven into the bed of the river. Driving the piles was completed on 5 June 1845 and the bridge was ready for opening less than five weeks later! Built into the abutments on both sides of the river was a side arch 7ft 9in wide, with an internal stairway giving access to a landing serving the public footpath across the bridge, which was situated between the tracks. At a later date, after the failure of some cast iron bridges, timber supports were put in to strengthen the bridge and at their outer ends the struts were held in cast iron shoes, some of which can still be seen.

In 1874, in connection with the building of the new station, the bridge was rebuilt in wrought iron, using the existing abutments and centre pier, but the footpath was moved to the south-east side of the bridge and external access stairs were provided. Alterations to the river bank at the station side meant the closure of the side arch, but at the other side of the river the arch is still in use and the walled-up entrance to the interior stairway can still be seen.

The NER architect during the planning stage was Thomas Prosser, but he retired in 1874 and the department was taken over by Benjamin Burleigh, who died in 1876; next on the scene was William Peachey and it was during his term of office that the station was completed and opened. However, mention should also be made of William Bell, the NER architect who succeeded Peachey in 1877 and who remained in office until 1914; he had started with the NER in 1857, working in

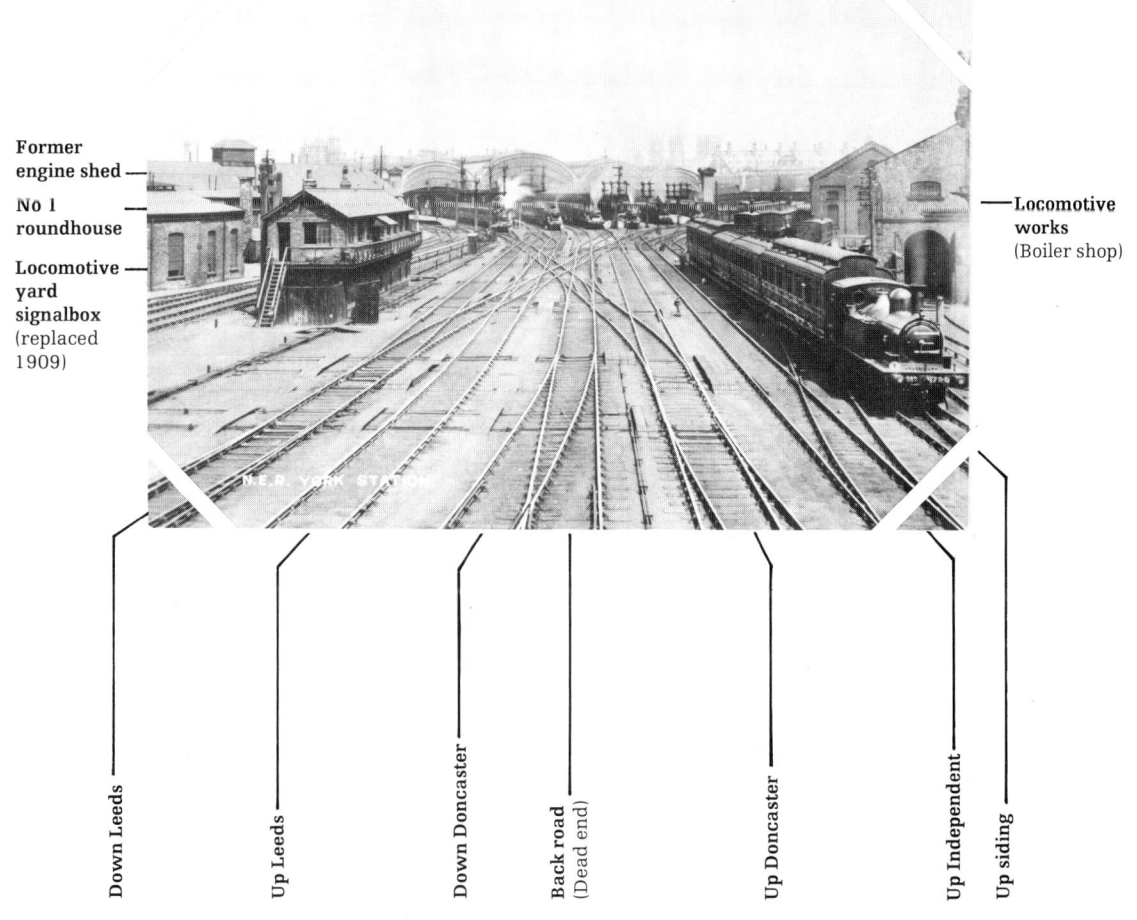

Former engine shed

No 1 roundhouse

Locomotive yard signalbox (replaced 1909)

Locomotive works (Boiler shop)

Down Leeds

Up Leeds

Down Doncaster

Back road (Dead end)

Up Doncaster

Up Independent

Up siding

York: Locomotive yard signalbox and South end of Station c1907.

Top: **The south end of the station in the 1950s. The platforms, from left to right, are 16, 15, 14, 11, 10, 9, 8, 3 and 2.** *E. Sanderson*

Above: **The south end of the station from Holgate Dock, using a telephoto lens, with the Minster and the NER Offices in the background.** *E. Sanderson*

Left: **The Tea Room and Cafe erected in 1906 near the end of the Scarborough bay platforms. Until recently it housed the Eastern Region's Relics Shop, approached from Tea Room Square outside the station.** *BR*

turn under his three predecessors, and he is recognised as having made a substantial contribution to the design of the new station.

In February 1874 construction of the station and the hotel was again put up for tender; plans and specifications could be obtained from Mr Burleigh on 16, 17 and 18 March and the completed tender had to be returned on the following day. For a task of this magnitude this ridiculously tight timetable proved too ambitious and the date for tenders was extended to 16 April. On the following day the Directors accepted the tender of John Keswick of York. However, in 1875 it was reported to the Board that work was not progressing satisfactorily and progress was slow due to strikes and differences between contractor and workmen. This led to the withdrawal of the contractor and the job was awarded to Lucas Brothers of London at a price of £187,468, with an additional £30,626 earmarked for engineering works.

The magnificent glazed train shed roof is 800ft long and consists of an 81ft span (48ft high) over the four centre tracks with a 55ft span (40ft high) on each side. On the east side of the station there is a 43ft span (36ft high) north and south of the station buildings. The wrought iron ribs of the roof are supported on cast iron columns. The brickwork is in yellow Scarborough brick, with stone dressings.

When the station opened it had 13 platforms — two through platforms, five bays at the south end and six at the north: in addition there were two tracks between the two main platform lines. An unusual feature was that although the two centre roads were known as 'Up Main' and 'Down Main' through the station, their designation changed when they emerged at the south end, the Up Main becoming 'Back Road' and terminating at buffer stops between Locomotive Yard and Holgate Bridge signalboxes, whilst the Down Main became the 'Up Leeds'. The 14th platform, shown in the 1871 plans as an Excursion Platform, was not built initially but appeared in 1900 as an extension to the station to handle the crowds expected at the Royal Agricultural Show held at York in that year. At the same time a footbridge was erected between platforms 4 and 5 to supplement the subway which had sufficed since 1877. An 1871 scheme submitted to the NER was for 'a gangway worked by hydraulic power' to join the two main platforms.

Originally the platforms at the south end extended only a short distance beyond the overall roof but they were extended twice, the last

occasion in 1909 bringing the length of No 4 platform (now No 8) to 1,692ft and No 5 (now No 9) to 1,575ft. Before going any further I should point out that from 20 September 1938 10 of the 13 original platforms were renumbered, and 15 and 16 added: originally the platforms had been numbered 1, 2, 3, 6 and 7 at the south end of the station and 8-13 at the north end, with 4 and 5 the up and down through platforms, and No 14 outside the west wall. To simplify matters it was decided to have the low numbers 1-8 on the east side of the station and 9-16 on the west side. The equivalents were:

New	Old
1*	1
2	2
3	3
4	13
5	12
6	11
7	10
8	4
9	5
10	6
11	7
12	9
13	8
14	14
15	—
16	—

*No 1 Platform abolished 1966

Henceforward, to avoid confusion, the new numbers will be used irrespective of period. As platforms 8 and 9 can accommodate two trains they were at some time divided into 8S and 8N, and 9S and 9N, but they became 8A and 8B, and 9A and 9B respectively in May 1975 as it had been found that some passengers were confused by the north and south suffixes, expecting a train standing at 8S or 9S to depart for the south, and a train at 8N or 9N to depart for the north — which was not always so.

When the station was opened in 1877 the Anglo-Scottish traffic had begun to develop and the East Coast Joint Stock services between London and Scotland were well established. However, the first British dining car did not appear until 1879 — and not on the East Coast services until 1893; even then the facility was provided only on one train in each direction. Consequently the main East Coast expresses — notably the 10.00am from King's Cross — had to

make an extended halt at York to allow the passengers to obtain sustenance — solid or liquid — and large dining and refreshment rooms were established on Platform 8. This was then the only platform that could be used by up trains, but the layout was so arranged and signalled that down expresses also used No 8 to stop conveniently for the refreshment facilities without the need for passengers to stampede through the subway. Thus the timetable shows the 10.00am from King's Cross stopping at York from 1.55pm to 2.25pm, and the 10.00am from Edinburgh from 2.35pm to 3.05pm. I wonder what happened if the down train was running late and two trainloads of passengers descended on the refreshment rooms at the same time?

In 1900, with the introduction of dining cars on the 10.00am trains, the stop was cut to 10 minutes for changing engines and this was carried out at the recently opened Platform 14. At first No 14 could be used only in the down direction, but with the opening of the new Locomotive Yard signalbox in 1909 it was converted to a single line, worked without a tablet or staff, but with the signals at each end electrically interlocked. In 1938, when No 15 platform was brought into use, a similar arrangement was adopted until the new electric signalling was completed.

In 1906 a Tea Room was erected on Platform 8; in World War 2 this became the Staff

Above: **In the 1930s the Chief Area Engineer, John Miller, made a determined attempt to brighten the lineside by laying lawns, planting shrubs, and surrounding the plots with concrete edging made by the LNER at York. An improvement of this kind can be seen in this view of the formal cutting of the first sod for station extensions (Platforms 15 and 16), which took place on 9 July 1936. The ceremony was performed by Thos Hornsby, Divisional General Manager (with spade) who was introduced by John Miller (behind the spade).** *BR*

Above right: **Work in progress on Platforms 15 and 16 in February 1938. The former 'Midland' shed can be seen in the right background.** *BR*

Right: **An aerial photograph of York taken by a German pilot on 4 October 1939, one month after the outbreak of war. This lists railway targets ranging from 'Werkstatthalle für Personenwagen' — Carriage Works — to 'Wasserturm' — water tower.**
Author's collection

Canteen, although it had a spell as the temporary booking office. Now it is the Eastern Region Stores Department's Relics Shop, with the entrance from Tea Room Square outside the station.

On 9 July 1936 the formal cutting of the first sod took place for the extensions on the west side of the station. A new island platform 1,180ft long was to be erected, forming Platforms 15 and 16

and to reach these the barrow subway was to be extended below ground and the passenger foot-bridge above ground. The footbridge was not in its original position, having been moved a few yards to the north when it was desired to install barriers and ticket collection facilities in 1930. Plat-form 15 opened for traffic on 3 April 1938 as the first phase of a scheme not only to enlarge the station but also to resignal the whole of the station with colour light signals and power operated points. However, work on the resignalling had to cease in 1939 because of the outbreak of World War 2, and both the extensions and the resignal-ling were not completed until 1951.

In October 1946, as part of its postwar improvement scheme, the LNER announced that the footbridge would be replaced by a subway, and another postwar scheme which came to nothing was to join up the tracks serving the bays at the south end (Nos 2 and 3) with those at the north end (Nos 6 and 7) to give two additional through platforms.

In December 1941 the geographical system of window allocation at the booking office was changed to an alphabetical system, with the three main windows allocated to stations A to K+Leeds and London; L to Z+Leeds and London; and Navy, Army and RAF: other windows were spare to handle bookings at rush periods. Only a few months later the booking office was destroyed by

Left: The effects of the bombing on 29 April 1942, with the Parcels Office completely destroyed, the Booking Office gutted, and the station roof badly damaged. *BR*

Below: Platform 15 was opened on 3 April 1938 but work on No 16 was left incomplete because of World War 2. Here 'V2' No 917 is pulling out of the extended Platform 14 and it can be seen from the layout that although Platform 15 could be used for through trains Platform 16 could not, when this view was taken in February 1948. *Author's collection*

Left: A station pilot of c1885. No 966 was a Class 964 0-6-0ST built by Robert Stephenson & Co in 1875, standing in old No 13 platform (now No 4). It was withdrawn from York shed in 1906 and sold in the following year to the Seaton Burn Coal Co in Northumberland, where it ran for a further 20 years. *LPC*

fire after the German bombing raid when an incendiary bomb fell on the nearby lamp room, in which were stored 500 gallons of paraffin! The attack came in the early hours of 29 April 1942, with the 10.15pm King's Cross-Edinburgh sleeping car train standing at Platform 9; some of the coaches were set on fire and although a number of coaches were removed by shunters and train crews six coaches had to be left at the platform and they were totally destroyed, leaving only the bogies, underframes, and vestibule frames. The buildings adjoining the lamp room were destroyed; a temporary parcels office was set up in the Refreshment Room and a booking office in the former Tea Room. Fortunately the fittings and ticket stock from the Booking Office were rescued during the raid and carried across the road to the moat at the foot of the City walls!

The most damaged platforms were Nos 1, 2 and 3, and at the inner end of No 3 one of the roof columns was completely destroyed by a high-explosive bomb: a large baulk of timber provided a temporary support, but later a new cast iron column was fitted and this can still be located because if lacks the decorative acanthus leaves at the top of the column as cast on the original. Traffic was moving again by the evening of the same day, and 24 hours later all running lines were available for traffic. However, permanent repairs to the roof were not completed until many years later.

During repairs to the roof in 1953 the contractors, John Butler & Co of Stanningley (a branch of the family firm which had erected the original roof in 1877) had to remove some of the so-called NER coats-of-arms incorporated in the cast iron supports. Two of these were restored to their correct heraldic colours and one was retained by the BR District Engineer and the other by the contractors. In 1971, during a partial repainting of the station to mark the 1900th anniversary of the City of York, it was decided to treat similarly some of the remaining coats-of-arms adjacent to the footbridge, and at other locations where they can easily be seen by passengers. By that time the District Engineer was Mr M. F. Barbey, who was interested in heraldry as a hobby, and under his guidance the shields were painted in their correct colours.

The heraldic badges on the spandrels consist of coats-of-arms appropriated by the three main constituent companies — the York & North Midland, York, Newcastle & Berwick, and the Leeds Northern — which amalgamated in 1854 to form the North Eastern Railway. None of these companies was authorised by the College of Heralds to use the designs they had adopted, nor indeed was the North Eastern, which extensively used the combined version. The heraldic devices, therefore, are not true coats-of-arms but merely badges — in fact little more than trade marks!

In the circulating area the NER tile map was for a time covered by a poster as it was considered out of date, but in 1969, with the realisation of its historic interest, the map was revealed and is worthy of inspection. The greatest disappointment, which meets the eye as one enters past the enquiry office, is the W. H. Smith's bookstall with its drab and boarded frontage giving the appearance that it is closed. What a difference from the old open bookstall which gave life and colour to the circulating area.

Lighting at the station was initially by gas; the NER opened its own gasworks at Gasworks Junction (later Severus Junction and York Yard North) on 31 December 1868, and a small power station was opened on the west side of the station in 1891, primarily for supplying incandescent lamps at the Royal Station Hotel. A much larger power station was erected on Leeman Road in 1901 and this had six boilers 28ft long by 7ft diameter; when the station closed in 1925 five of these were sent to LNER sleeper depots for conversion into creosoting cylinders — two to Hartlepool and three to Lowestoft.

On 14 February 1957 gas lighting on the platforms was abolished and a change made to electricity using the cold cathode system. This was formally switched on by the Lord Mayor of York, but the system was replaced in 1975 using a sodium installation which gives a high standard of lighting throughout the station.

In 1970 it was found that the wood and glass endscreens of the roof spans were rotten and Planning Permission was obtained to replace all eight in aluminium and glass at an estimated cost of £35,000. A start was made in 1972 and the task was completed in the following year. The new screens successfully retain the appearance of the old and the difference can only be distinguished by close inspection.

Early in 1975 TV screens were installed alongside the departure indicators, at the ticket barriers, and at other strategic locations; these display details of the running of trains, giving their booked time of arrival, platform, and, if running late, the estimated time of arrival. This useful system replaced a manually operated arrangement using a number of boards in a large frame mounted at the south end of the former

Right: The most familiar station pilots were the 'J71' 0-6-0T engines and this is No 495 at Clifton. The signal controlling the down main line was one of the first upper quadrant signals at York. *W. Potter*

Below: The south end of the station in the 1960s with the end screens awaiting renewal. *BR*

Above: The north end of the station in 1973, with the reglazing of the end screens completed. *BR*

Left: A High Speed Train arriving at Platform 9 viewed from the footbridge. *BR*

Right: The lighting of the platforms was changed from gas to electric in 1957, with an improved standard of illumination. *E. Sanderson*

Below: Restoring in their correct heraldic colours the cast iron versions of the NER coat-of-arms incorporated in the spandrels of the station roof. Those close to the footbridge, and others easily visible to passengers were so treated in 1971.   *BR*

Platform signalbox. The train departure indicators currently in use are based on the pattern introduced by the NER at its larger stations, the main difference being that the roll is now moved forward electrically simply by a member of the staff pressing a button, whereas the original design relied on a man turning on the roll by means of a crank handle. A public address system was first used in 1927.

The inability of the original station to handle any extra traffic led to the building of two excursion platforms immediately south of Holgate Bridge. These were originally built for the passengers attending a Review of Volunteers held on 28 September 1860. At that time there were only two tracks south of York station and the platforms were erected on two loops, one on each side of the running lines. With the opening of the new station and two additional tracks to the south, the excursion platforms were moved outwards on to two new loops and they remained in this position until demolished in 1964.

The platforms were regularly used for special events on the Knavesmire (the scene of the Pope's recent visit to York), but the main use was for York Races and they were last used for this purpose on 24 August 1939. There is a strong possibility that the platforms were used for some trains after the bombing of the City in April 1942, but in spite of enquiries among local staff this has

Above: **In 1975 an even better standard of illumination was achieved by changing to sodium lighting. 'Deltic' No 55.014 is standing at Platform 9 on the 00.05 King's Cross-Newcastle at four o'clock in the morning! Exposure was 1 minute at F16 using Kodak Tri-X film. Note the NER Co casting, originally made for a semaphore signal gantry, in use with the colour-light gantry.** *W. K. Watson*

Above right: **Midnight at York. Another night shot, looking across from Platform 8 to No 9, with No 55.007 on the 20.15 King's Cross-Edinburgh, due in York at one minute to midnight — and the station clock actually shows 00.02! Both night shots were taken in October 1981 when the end was in sight for the notable 'Deltic' locomotives. Exposure was again 1 minute at F11.** *W. K. Watson*

Right: **Steam locomotives at York attract large audiences! This is 19** *Bittern* **bound for Scarborough on 16 September 1972.** *BR*

not been confirmed. However, the down platform was used on 23 June 1957 by passengers joining a Railway Correspondence & Travel Society rail tour, which then used the 1841 route through York to rejoin the main line to the north at Skelton Junction.

Although not actually using the platforms at Holgate Bridge some trains ran via York Yard when engineering works were taking place between York station and Skelton. Up trains

stopped at Holgate and a pilot engine was used to draw the train back into the station, with the train engine remaining coupled in the rear, ready to set off for the south as soon as station duties had been completed.

In World War 1 the down Holgate platform was cut away at the north end to allow egress from the new reception sidings, but the same platform was extended at the south end to compensate. An annual feature on the up platform was 'Y O R K' in flowers planted out by the BR staff from the nursery at Poppleton.

As the primitive signalling improved, and signalboxes became necessary to control the signals and points from a central position, boxes were established at the three ends of the triangle of lines outside the 1841 station. It will be remembered that the station was a terminus with lines from north and south joining just outside the City Walls, and thus just outside the station. Here Archway box was built, obviously so named because of its proximity to the Andrews arch through the Walls. Joining the two lines from north and south and providing a through route without entering the station, forming the third side of the triangle, was the line from North Junction (on the main line to the north) to Holgate Junction (on the main line to the south). Over the years this box was also known as Holgate Junction and Holgate Bridge Junction.

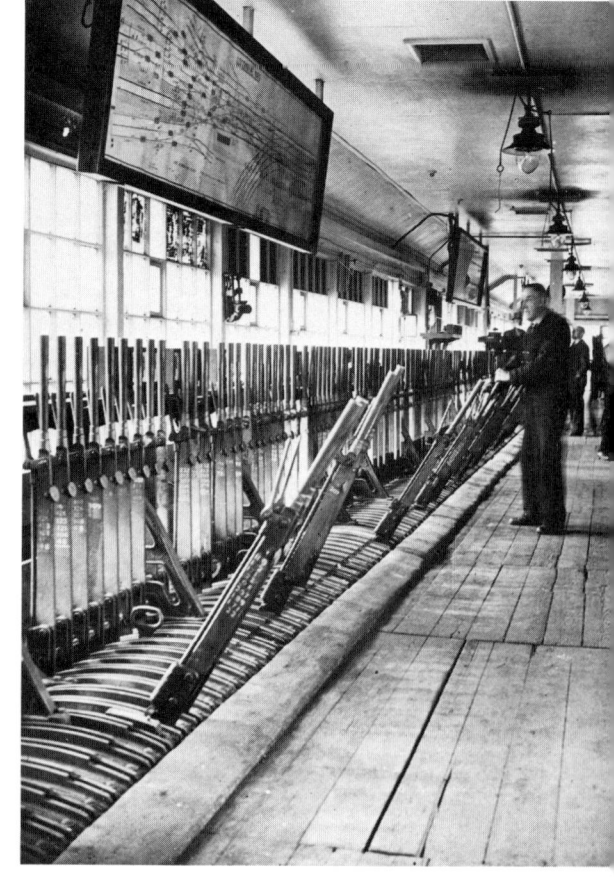

North Junction also controlled the junction with the Scarborough branch but from the station direction this could be gained only by a reversal. Thus Scarborough bound trains were usually propelled out of the station and then, when over the junction, the engine reversed and set off for Scarborough; on occasions a spare engine hauled the train to the junction, with the train engine on the rear. All that was necessary at North Junction was for the leading engine to uncouple and the train engine could then depart with the train for the coast. Reversal, outside the station, although not operationally necessary, was also carried out with the Scotch expresses from the north, which at North Junction took the curve to Holdgate Junction and then reversed into the station to keep the train the same way round when ready to leave for the south.

At a very early stage the Great Northern was complaining about the inadequacy of the station and over the years a number of accidents took place due to the restricted space and the practice of reversing trains into and out of the station. In fact the Inspecting Officer stated that there was not much that could be done to alleviate the position and that it would have to be endured until the new station, then under construction, was ready.

When the new station was finally opened in 1877 the south end was controlled by Locomotive

Above left: In November 1977 the famous *Flying Scotsman* engine was disguised in various forms for a film based on the life of Agatha Christie. Here it is at Platform 7 as No 4480 *Enterprise* — although on the other side it is No 4474 *Victor Wild*! The number on the front buffer beam was changed from 4474 to 4480 as required. *BR*

Signalboxes

Above: Locomotive Yard box on 11 May 1951, with work going ahead in preparation for the change to electric signalling nine days later. The box was demolished immediately after closure to allow the new layout to be completed the following weekend, including linking up the tracks approaching the box at front and end in the above view. *BR*

Left: The interior of Locomotive Yard box with its 295 lever frame. The first lever visible on the left is No 23 and they were arranged in two sections, 1 to 145 and 146 to 295. The gap in the centre allowed the signalman in charge of the box access to the covered balcony for verbal communication with the shunters etc. *BR*

Yard box, with Holgate Bridge Box, a short distance to the south, controlling the junction with the curve to North Junction. Holgate Bridge box was a very tall structure to enable the signalman to look south over Holgate Bridge; it was situated on the up side of the line north of the bridge and it was removed in 1909 when the whole of the south

end working was taken over by the new Locomotive Yard box. From 1900, with the opening of Platform 14, the old Locomotive Yard box had 129 levers and Holgate Bridge had 46.

When the line to Selby was opened in 1871 it branched off the Normanton line at Chandler's Whin Junction, two miles south of York station, but in 1877 two additional running lines were provided from the station and trains were routed to their appropriate tracks at Locomotive Yard, allowing Chandler's Whin Junction to be removed. Intermediate boxes remained at North Lane, to control a level crossing, and at South Points, which controlled the entrance and exit of the platform loops at Holgate. In May 1900 the box and junction at Chaloner Whin (a new version of the name!) were reinstated to ease the situation when handling the extra traffic expected for the Royal Show, for which Platform 14 was provided. At the same time plans were being prepared for doubling from Chaloner Whin to Church Fenton and this was completed in 1904, giving the layout we know today, although now all points and signals are operated from the electric box opened in 1951. Incidentally, under LNER ownership, when the NER pattern enamelled signalbox nameplates were removed and replaced by the LNER pattern wooden boards, Chaloner Whin became Chaloners Whin.

In 1902 powers were obtained to close North

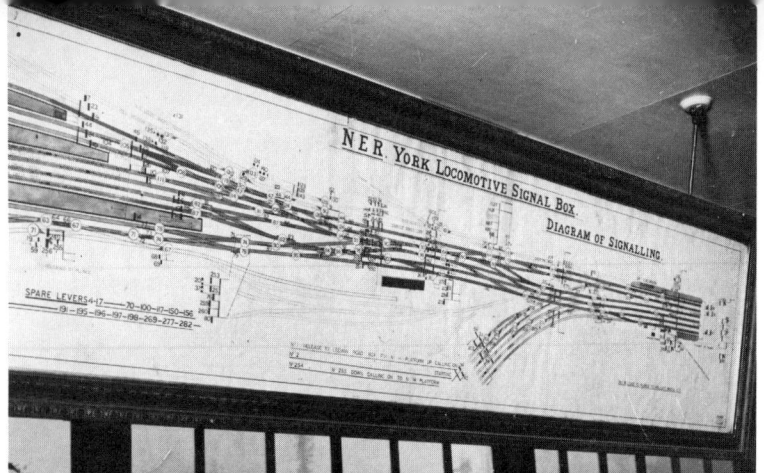

Left: The diagram in Locomotive Yard box, although it mistakenly carries the title Locomotive Box. The name Locomotive Yard originated when the Old Station was in use (ie prior to 1877) and was retained even though the major locomotive depot was later established north of the station. *BR*

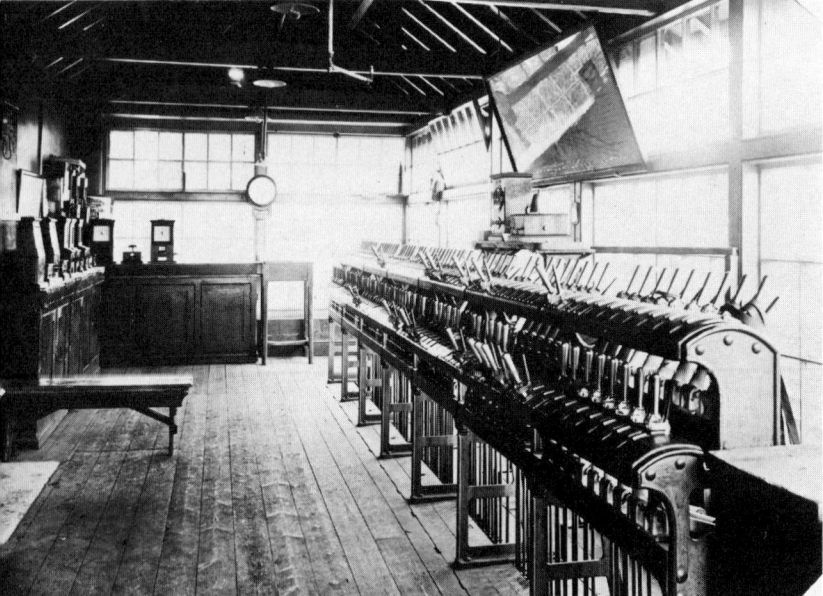

Centre left: The old manual box at Severus Junction was demolished on 19 and 20 September 1903 and on the following day the operation of points and signals was taken over by a power box using the 'Crewe' system, with a frame only 21ft 10½in long housing 133 levers (91 working and 42 spare).

This frame was removed in 1922 and a 150-lever mechanical frame fitted, which required the extension of the existing box. In its lengthened form the box still exists but has been disfigured by the fitting of a flat roof to allow a new road to go over the top.
Crown Copyright, National Railway Museum, York

Bottom left: Holgate platforms were a convenient location for photography, especially for up trains. This is 'B17' No 2832 *Belvoir Castle* on an up express running on the Up Doncaster line. This became the Up Normanton line at Chaloners Whin Junction, where the Doncaster line diverged; thus it was operationally preferable to use the Up Doncaster/Up Normanton line for trains taking the old Y&NM route at Church Fenton, for Knottingley, Swinton & Knottingley Joint line, or Normanton, to avoid as far as possible crossing trains from one route to the other. For the same reason Leeds expresses were usually routed on the up and down Leeds lines, but as the stations between York and Church Fenton were served only by the Normanton lines it was necessary to run stopping trains for Leeds on the Normanton line, crossing them to the Micklefield route at Church Fenton. However, in the event of out of course running the fast trains taking either route could use which tracks were most suitable, sometimes crossing from one to the other and back again to overtake a laggardly freight train, or a train with a failed locomotive.
Real Photographs

Lane level crossing and to replace it with a bridge a short distance to the south (St Helen's Road) and this led to the closure of North Lane box. However, in World War 1 extensive siding accommodation was provided on the up side of the line at Dringhouses and to control the exit from these sidings a new box named Dringhouses was provided a hundred yards north of the site of North Lane box. However, Dringhouses box was closed on 30 September 1928 and the exit points electrically worked from Chaloners Whin box.

Also in World War 1 a set of four reception sidings was provided behind the down Holgate platform, with the entrance controlled by the conveniently placed South Points box. Originally passengers detraining at the down Holgate Excursion Platform walked up the slope directly on to Holgate Road, but to allow an outlet from the north end of the sidings a footbridge had to be built. The outlet was controlled from a new box named Holgate Bridge, although it was actually classed as a Ground Frame, controlled electrically from Locomotive Yard box.

The crossovers and signals in the centre of the station were controlled by Platform box, with 80 levers, which closed when the new box was opened in 1951. It was situated at the rear of the circulating area, with the bookstall underneath. Since closure as a signalbox the cabin has been used as a convenient base for the Assistant Stationmasters and Inspectors in charge of the station on three shifts, with a battery of telephones to receive information regarding the running of trains, and to issue instructions etc.

The north end of the station was controlled by Waterworks box alone (with 132 levers) until in 1900 Leeman Road box (with 91 levers) was added to control the exit from Platfrom 14, and to take over control of the two adjacent platforms, now 12 and 13. Waterworks box was demolished in 1938 to allow the tracks from York Yard South and Platform 14 to the Scarborough branch to be re-arranged.

In the 1938 alterations only two tracks across the main line were to be provided, still crossing on the level but serving the goods traffic and Platforms 14, 15 and 16. To obtain the best course these two tracks were realigned to run across the site of the original Waterworks box, which was replaced by a temporary wooden box to the north. The 'temporary' box lasted until 1951, when Leeman Road was also demolished.

Further north Clifton box originally controlled the main lines and the exit from the 'new' engine sheds; the carriage sidings on both sides of the line were not provided until many years later. When the sidings on the down side were installed about 1900 an occupation overbridge leading from Leeman Road to the river bank had to be demolished but the abutment on the up side was left until the sidings on that side were provided some years later. It was in this area that Dr Budden spent some time photographing trains leaving York for the north around the turn of the century, and some of his views actually show the bridge in place; others show the one surviving abutment on the up side, and later views show the abutment removed and Clifton Carriage Sidings covering the site. With the extension of the engine shed at the north end of the station a new Clifton box, with 120 levers, was provided c1915 and this box remained in use until 1951.

Back at the south end of the station the most notable event was the opening of the new Locomotive Yard box on 6 June 1909; this had 295 levers and it was situated south of the previous box of the same name. The frame was manufactured by McKenzie & Holland to the requirements of A. Hurst, the NER Southern Division Signal Engineer, and although the signals were to the standard NER pattern the locking was unusual. The switch of the facing points was held close to the stock rail by means of a steel wedge worked by the signal lever, and to this wedge was attached the wire operating the signal itself. Unless the switch was a good fit tight up to the stock rail the wedge could not be placed in its locking position and thus the signal remained at danger. On one occasion in 1922 a piece of equipment was accidentally dropped in the points and held them partly open, and although the wedge was not in position the play and wear in the rodding allowed the signal to be cleared, leading to a derailment.

Staff access to Locomotive Yard box and the locomotive sheds at the south end of the station was provided by a footbridge from the Queen Street locomotive works area which crossed all the running lines. This bridge was also used as a signal gantry and carried a number of posts. Until 1909 the old Locomotive Yard box was some distance north of the footbridge, but the new box was immediately south of the bridge. The footbridge proved an excellent vantage point for railway photographers recording trains leaving the south end of the station, notably in the 1920s and 1930s, but it was demolished as a result of the colour light signals installation in 1951.

With the opening of the new station in 1877 the area adjoining the old main line north of North

Junction, as far as Severus Junction (originally Gasworks Junction), became known as York Yard, with tracks and sidings on the west side serving the carriage works, and on the east serving the wagon works, Leeman Road goods warehouse, and private sidings. In October 1938, after almost a century's existence, North Junction box was renamed York Yard South. A new electrically operated box was opened in September 1962.

Proceeding north through the yard there were at one time five boxes controlling the exit from various groups of sidings — No 1 Down Goods, No 2 Down Goods, No 1 Up Goods, No 2 Up Goods, and No 3 Up Goods — before Severus Junction was reached. At Severus Junction the new main line from the 1877 station, after two lengthy reverse curves, rejoined the 1841 Great North of England formation, but there does not appear to have been any physical connection between the two routes until Poppleton Junction was reached, $\frac{1}{2}$-mile to the north, where the box also controlled the junction with the Harrogate branch. From 21 September 1903 a new box was provided at Severus Junction using compressed air on the Crewe system. This lasted until 1922 when the box was lengthened and a manual frame was re-introduced. The box became York Yard North in October 1938 and at the same time Poppleton Junction was renamed Skelton Junction; the latter was replaced by an all electric installation in June 1941. During World War 2 additional sidings were provided at Government expense on the down side north of the Harrogate branch junction, together with a 70ft turntable and coaling and watering facilities to ease the work on the locomotive depot. These sidings have now been removed and in 1977 the Harrogate branch connection was remodelled to provide only a single connection off the down main line; up trains use the same connection and then a cross-over to the Up Main.

The scheme to electrify all the signals in the York area was announced in 1936 and the contract was awarded to the Westinghouse Brake & Signal Co Ltd in the following year, for what would be the largest route relay interlocking installation in the world. This involved the closure of Chaloners Whin, South Points, Locomotive Yard, Platform, Waterworks, Leeman Road and Clifton manual boxes. The area covered by the new box involves $33\frac{1}{4}$ track miles and uses 317 track circuits, allowing a total of 828 separate routes to be set up. The running signals are of the 3 or 4 aspect type depending on the speed of trains at each location, with route indicators of various types at diverging junctions. Subsidiary signals under running signals are illuminated only when cleared and show two white lights at an angle of 45 degrees. The same clear indication is given by the 154 shunting signals, which normally display a red and a white light set horizontally for 'stop'. Except for a few sets of points at outlying locations the point layouts are worked electro-pneumatically; the others are worked by electric point motors.

The new box, with its extensive illuminated control panel, is built between Platforms 13 and 14, just to the north of the footbridge. The train announcer is housed in a cubicle overlooking the panel, and although observation windows are provided on both sides of the box these are not used as it is possible to obtain a far better indication of the state of things from the panel rather than by visual observation through the windows! Each of the four panels is manned by one signalman, with a Regulator in control.

A stand-by generator set is provided in case of failure of the mains supply and this is brought into use automatically in eight seconds. Duplicate electrically driven air compressors are provided to supply the points; the main set maintains the pressure at between 55 and 65lb/sq in and if the pressure drops to 53lb the stand-by set will also cut in.

One improvement on the manually signalled layout is that the Up Main line through the station, together with Nos 8, 9, 14, 15 and 16 platform lines can be used in either direction. This has proved to be invaluable at busy times and I noted one occasion when it was most effectively used. A train from the south, bound for Scarborough was standing in Platform 9, where it was due to change engines. The replacement engine was already standing waiting on the Down Main but difficulty was being experienced in uncoupling the incoming engine and the down non-stop was approaching. No 14 platform was also blocked but fortunately the Up Main was clear and the non-stop, with *Merlin* in charge, was routed through the station on the Up Main. The Down Main is not available in both directions.

Because of the 15 year delay between the initiation and completion of the York signalling scheme much of the apparatus was out of date before the box opened in 1951. The relays, for instance, were gigantic when compared with today's relays, but the box has already given 30 years service and looks good for a few years yet, especially considering the financial situation in

Right: The interesting gantry of semaphore signals has gone as 'V2' No 60814 heads south in 1956. *Author*

Below: Probably the last passenger train to stop at Holgate Platforms was this RCTS rail-tour headed by 'D20' No 62387, which ran in June 1957. *C. Ord*

Bottom: Raven Atlantic No 733 passing the outlet at the south end of Dringhouses sidings. The signalbox in the background was closed in 1928 and subsequently demolished. *C. Ord*

Left: Chaloners Whin Junction looking south, with the Doncaster line diverging on the left; Normanton lines on the left and Leeds lines on the right. Milepost 2, from a Zero in the centre of York station, just beyond the box. *BR*

Below: The old layout at the north end of the station, with the goods lines crossing the main line north of Waterworks box; the view is looking towards Scarborough Bridge. Waterworks box had 132 levers in two frames, and Leeman Road box had 91 levers. Prior to the opening of Leeman Road box in 1900 the vacancies for three signalmen were notified to the staff, offering a wage of £1 8s (£1.40) per week. *BR*

Right: Looking in the opposite direction — from Scarborough Bridge — with the goods lines curving round to the north of Waterworks box to cross the main lines on the level. The bays on the left are now Platforms 4, 5, 6 and 7 and the 'J71' pilot is standing at 8N, now 8B. *BR*

which BR finds itself. The box must have paid for itself over and over again, not only because of the seven manual boxes which it replaced, but also in the speed and flexibility of operation, with routes being set up and the signals cleared without stopping a train approaching the controlling signal.

In April 1960 British Railways announced its intention of introducing Centralised Traffic Control between York and Beverley and in May 1961 stated that the contract had been awarded to the Westinghouse Brake & Signal Co. The scheme involved the singling of $31\frac{1}{2}$ miles of double track, leaving double track connections some 1,000yd long approaching the junctions at Bootham (York) and Beverley, with passing loops at Pocklington ($\frac{3}{4}$-mile long) and Market Weighton ($1\frac{1}{4}$ miles long). Automatically controlled half-barriers were to be installed at 19 level crossings. A new console in the signalbox at York would have an illuminated diagram of the line, with thumb switches for the operation of points and signals and for the control of Ground Frames and the three manned level crossings. It was expected that the project, one of the largest CTC installations in the country, would enable considerable economies to be made in the

operation of traffic over the line, as well as in maintenance and renewal. As a pilot scheme it would also furnish valuable information and experience on which to establish the place of CTC in BR's Modernisation Plan — according to a BR Press Release! It was also stated that 'The plan is unique to this country and can be regarded as a pilot scheme for the country in general. The economic gain was such that lines could be altered which otherwise might well have to close down'. However, the fine plan was all to no avail. Although the material was ordered — and much of it delivered — the scheme failed to save the Beverley line because it closed in November 1965 without acquiring 'the Continental look' envisaged in the BR announcement.

The closure of the Beverley line did not affect the manual box at Bootham Junction, 1 mile 55c from York, which had to remain open to operate the level crossing gates for Wigginton Road, and the box at Burton Lane, 1 mile 4c from York, still opens to handle the traffic to and from the Foss Islands branch.

In May 1964 the North Eastern Region brought into use the first private microwave radio telephone link in the British Isles, between York, Darlington and Newcastle. This enabled direct

dialling to be used between some 3,000 railway extensions as far apart as Leeds and Berwick. The system was installed by Marconi Ltd and the York installation necessitated a large 'dish' aerial mounted on a 46ft lattice steel tower on top of the former North Eastern offices. From York the signal was beamed to a repeater station 850ft above sea level at Woolmoor, four miles north-east of Thirsk. Further aerials were provided at Darlington, Ferryhill and Tyne Yard. Initially the system catered for a maximum of 159 channels but this could be increased to 300 channels when warranted.

This installation was complementary to the automatic telephone exchange, with seven manual positions for incoming calls, installed in the NER office building in 1959.

When the new hotel opened in 1878 the hotel dating from 1853 at the old station was closed, and at a sale in June 1878 the contents were sold by auction. The furniture and fittings from 15 reception rooms and 55 bedrooms, together with 2,200 items of silver plate, assorted oil paintings and engravings, were divided into more than 2,000 lots and realised £2,516 9s. Connections were then made between the old hotel and the

station offices on one side, and between the hotel and the refreshment room block on the other, giving additional office space which is still in use today.

As the North Eastern continued to grow yet more office accommodation was required and Scawin's Hotel (adjacent to the entrance to the old station from Tanner Row) was taken over, £1,079 15s 4d being expended to convert it into offices. Then came the major decision to build a completely new office block on the site facing the old station hotel, including the plot occupied by the former Scawin's Hotel. In March 1899 the nearby North Eastern Hotel (on the opposite side of Tanner Row) came on the market and was purchased by the NER to house the staff in the Scawin's Hotel building which had to be demolished to make way for the new offices. The former North Eastern Hotel, now No 37 Tanner Row, has remained in railway ownership and now houses the District Control and the office of the Area Manager.

In its 1899 Act the North Eastern obtained powers for the compulsory purchase of 'certain lands situate between Station Road and Tanner Row, on the north-east side of the Company's road

Above left: An early BR view as 'A3' No 60045 *Lemberg* leaves Platform 9 for Newcastle, and a new 'B1' backs down to the station. Note the mixture of semaphore and colour light signals. Leeman Road box to the left and the temporary Waterworks box to the right. *K. C. Appleby collection*

Above: The interior of the electric box, opened on 20 May 1951. The cost of the scheme was £562,000! *BR*

Right: A signalling school was opened at York in October 1930, with a 1¼in gauge layout. In the centre is the quarter-size 25-lever frame controlling the single line and double line junctions depicted on the diagram, all correctly signalled. *Author's collection*

Exhibitions

Top: The station was the site for exhibitions of locomotives and rolling stock, with a small admission charge to help railway charities. The first was held in June 1928 and among the exhibits in the Scarborough bays were 'Y3' Sentinel shunter No 81 and 'K3' No 39. *H. G. W. Household*

Above: In October 1934 the largest engine on display was 'P2' No 2002 *Earl Marischal*, then only a few days old. *Author's collection*

Right: The centenary of the station was marked in June 1977 by a display of old and new items in Platforms 4, 5 and 6. In Platform 5 is 'Deltic' No 55.012 *Crepello* and in Platform 6 'A4' No 4468 *Mallard* from the National Railway Museum. *E. Sanderson*

adjoining the York Old Station' for the new offices and a fine building it turned out to be, with no expense spared. The outline design was by the company's architect William Bell, and the detail design was by consultant architect Horace Field.

Work started in March 1900 and the building was completed and opened on 20 September 1906: it was described at the time as 'a model of substantial construction and while the dominant idea is a matter-of-fact business place, elegance and artistic effects have never been forogtten'. The area occupied by the building is 2,750 sq yd and the length is 275ft. The floor space is 31,500 sq ft and the accommodation comprises 183 rooms. Some five million bricks were used in the construction of the building, including hand-made facing bricks from Sudbury in Suffolk. Accommodation is provided on five floors, with strong rooms and muniment rooms in the basement, together with boiler room and telephone exchange.

The Board Room in the west wing is a magnificent room 51ft by 28ft and 17ft high, with portraits of former North Eastern directors and officials on the panelled walls; unfortunately it is not now used for its original purpose. Electric lighting has been in use since the building was erected, originally using power supplied by the company's own generating station. The cost of the building was £72,100 5s 1d.

The tower on the east wing is surmounted by a large gilded weather vane, with the 'cock' in the form of a North Eastern locomotive. This is 128ft above the ground and at first a cut-out of a 'BTP' 0-4-4T was used, but in 1922 this was replaced by a Class S 4-6-0 (minus tender), the total length of engine and pointer being 7ft 6in. In 1962 a suggestion was made that modernisation and Nationalisation should take place by replacing the steam engine outline by one representing a diesel locomotive!

In York there are numerous buildings with railway connections and a few of the more notable are:

Holgate Villa: Thomas Cabry, the York & North Midland engineer, was provided with a large detached house, Holgate Villa, standing in its own grounds in Holgate Road; behind were the company's locomotive and wagon shops, with access from the back garden of the house. The house was subsequently occupied by various NER officials; it was let to private tenants, and finally occupied by

N.E.R.OFFICES

various railway departments, until it was demolished by British Railways and replaced by a modern office block in 1958.

44 Monkgate: In 1827 George Hudson inherited a large sum under the will of his great uncle, Matthew Botterill, and with it he purchased the property at 44 Monkgate, not far from the draper's business in College Street in which he was a partner. During his tempestuous career in the railway world he owned much larger houses and estates, such as Londesborough Park (near Market Weighton) and Newby Park (near Baldersby) purchased within a few weeks of one another in 1845. The house in Monkgate is now occupied by a firm of accountants.

Railway Institute: At its major centres the NER provided Institutes for the benefit of the staff; these included games rooms, handicraft rooms, lecture hall, library and other recreational facilities, and over the years they have been widely used and appreciated. The institute at York, situated between Queen Street bridge and the old Y&NM workshops, was opened in July 1899 and still flourishes.

Queen Street Bridge: Just outside the City Walls Queen Street crossed the lines into the old station on a level crossing. With the building of the new

Miscellaneous Buildings etc

Above: **The magnificent NER offices were opened in 1906 and recent cleaning of the brickwork and stonework has revealed the original beauty of the building. These prestige offices cost the North Eastern £72,100 5s 1d!** *Author's collection*

Above right: **The interior of the offices looking along one of the corridors.** *BR*

Right: **The nameplate at the door of the North Eastern offices when they were the headquarters of the North Eastern Region from 1 January 1948 to 31 December 1966. From 1 January 1967 they became the headquarters of the new Eastern Region, made up of the Eastern and North Eastern Regions. Thus the plate became redundant and is now in the author's possession.** *Author's collection*

station a better approach from Micklegate and Blossom Street became essential and in October 1877 W. D. Cameron of Leeds was awarded the contract for building a bridge to replace the level crossing; his price was £4,481. The bridge curves round with the walls and although the present structure does not give the impression of being particularly old one has only to look underneath

HEADQUARTERS
OFFICES

BRITISH
RAILWAYS

NORTH
EASTERN
REGION

to see that it is actually the original bridge strengthened and widened.

Holgate Bridge: In 1841 only two tracks passed under the original Holgate (or Holdgate) Bridge, although south of the bridge the tracks were increased to four with the building of the special platforms in 1860. In 1877, with the opening of the new station, there were four tracks from the station to the point of divergence of the Doncaster and Normanton lines at Chaloner Whin, requiring a new bridge at Holgate. The excursion platforms were moved outwards so that up and down loop lines could be maintained. It has been stated that these platforms were Ticket Platforms, so long favoured by the NER, but this was not so.

When electric trams were introduced in 1910, replacing the horsetrams, it was planned to run a service along Holgate Road to Acomb, but the existing bridge was found to be unsuitable and initially a service was provided only to the south end of the bridge (from 20 March 1910); on 9 June 1910 a service commenced from the north end of the bridge to Acomb, with passengers crossing the bridge on foot. In the same year York Corporation agreed to contribute £3,500 towards the cost of a new bridge and this was opened on 1 August 1911. At last a through tram service could commence. But this ceased in November 1935 when the West Yorkshire Road Car Co started to operate local services under the control of a committee on which the Corporation and the bus company were represented.

NER Laundry: In 1894 the North Eastern decided to build its own laundry for handling the linen from its hotels and refreshment rooms. It was built at Heworth, on the east side of the Foss Islands branch, with some 6,600sq ft of floor space. In 1929/30 it was enlarged to 14,000sq ft to handle four million items a year. It had its own siding for wagons bringing coal for the boilers, but transport of the linen between the station and the laundry was carried out by road. In 1982 it was announced that the laundry, together with another BR laundry at Edinburgh, had been sold.

LNER Garage: The NER opened a small garage for the benefit of visitors staying at the Royal Station Hotel, but this was rebuilt and enlarged by the LNER in 1924, resulting in the building in Leeman Road which exists today. It is faced with 'Atlas White' imitation stone.

Sorting Office: Adjoining the garage is the recently enlarged Post Office sorting office, connected to the station by a subway which passes under platforms 4, 5, 6 and 7, with access to Platform 8B by electric lifts.

War Memorial: Following the end of hostilities in 1918 the NER decided to erect a memorial to the memory of the employees who had been killed in the conflict, and Sir Edward Lutyens was commissioned to prepared a design. The site proposed was just inside the City Walls, at the end of the old Scarborough bay platforms, but there was some doubt about the suitability of the site when viewed from Lendal Bridge and a full-size wooden mock-up was erected. This was approved and on 1 December 1922 agreement was reached between the NER and York Corporation and construction commenced, although it was 14 June 1924 before the memorial was ready for unveiling. This was performed by Field Marshal Lord Plumer, in the presence of civic and church dignatories, NER and LNER directors, and relatives of the 2,236 men who died. The memorial consists of an obelisk of Portland stone, 54ft high, surrounded on three sides by stone screens 15ft high carrying the names of the fallen.

Right: **The statue by Milburn of George Leeman, Deputy Chairman of the NER from 1855 to 1874, and Chairman 1874 to 1880. He died on 25 February 1882 and is commemorated by this statue just outside the City Walls, within sight of the old and new stations and the 1906 offices.** *Author*

Below: **The North Eastern war memorial stands between the 1841 station and the City Walls, with Hudson House in the background. It was designed by Sir Edward Lutyens and was erected in memory of the North Eastern men killed in World War 1. The obelisk of Portland stone is 54ft high.** *Author*

Locomotive Allocations

Unfortunately official engine allocation lists have survived only from December 1923, but because of York's popularity with early railway photographers we have a photographic record of many of the old engines. Even so some of the smaller engines have gone unphotographed due, no doubt, to the photographers' desire to capture something new from Darlington or Gateshead rather than photograph an old locomotive which had been around for many years.

York Locomotive Allocation 6 December 1923

LNER Class	NER Class			
A7	Y	4-6-2T	(2)	1113, 1192
B15	S2	4-6-0	(7)	799, 813, 017, 020, 821, 822, 823 (Note 1)

Below: **Fletcher 2-2-2, built by R. & W. Hawthorn in 1861, at York shed coaling stage shortly after being reboilered in March 1886.** *LPC*

B16	S3	4-6-0	(28)	844, 845, 847, 848, 849, 908, 911, 921, 923, 925, 927, 933, 936, 942, 1371, 1374, 1377, 2364, 2366, 2368, 2370, 2372, 2373, 2374, 2376, 2378, 2380, 2382 (Note 2)
C6	V V/09	4-4-2	(4)	698, 699, 702, 1792
C7	Z	4-4-2	(15)	717, 721, 2163, 2164, 2165, 2166, 2167, 2168, 2169, 2171, 2172, 2198, 2199, 2202, 2208
D20	R	4-4-0	(15)	707, 708, 711, 713, 724, 1026, 1260, 1672, 2018, 2021, 2022, 2027, 2028, 2101, 2104
D21	R1	4-4-0	(7)	1237, 1238, 1239, 1240, 1241, 1245, 1246
—	901	2-4-0	(1)	910
—	1440	2-4-0	(1)	486

G6	BTP	0-4-4T	(3)	255, 466, 951
—	398	0-6-0	(3)	392, 1164, 1412
J21	C	0-6-0	(8)	34, 534, 807, 1516, 1803, 1804, 1807, 1809
J24	P	0-6-0	(1)	1844
J26	P2	0-6-0	(11)	412, 442, 525, 554, 818, 831, 1098, 1130, 1200, 1366, 1674
J27	P3	0-6-0	(5)	2342, 2343, 2354, 2355, 2383
J71	E	0-6-0T	(11)	237, 399, 447, 1084, 1085, 1134, 1140, 1163, 1167, 1758, 1831
J72	E1	0-6-0T	(9)	1746, 2307, 2309, 2313, 2328, 2331, 2332, 2333, 2334
J77	290	0-6-0T	(6)	138, 999, 1000, 1346, 1348, 1431 (Note 2)
X3	190	2-2-4T	(1)	1679

Ex-GN engines outstationed at York (1924 numbers)

C1	—	4-4-2	(2)	4424, 4447
D2	—	4-4-0	(8)	4180, 4331, 4386, 4387, 4390, 4396, 4398 (and one not identified)
D3	—	4-4-0	(2)	4071, 4348

Notes:
1 One unidentified engine of this class outstationed at Scarborough.
2 One unidentified engine of this class outstationed at Normanton.

York Locomotive Allocation 31 December 1932

A7	4-6-2T	(3)	1113, 1174, 1193
B13	4-6-0	(1)	775
B15	4-6-0	(8)	787, 797, 799, 813, 817, 820, 821, 822
B16	4-6-0	(19)	844, 847, 908, 923, 926, 927, 1373, 1377, 2364, 2366, 2368, 2370, 2371, 2372, 2373, 2374, 2376, 2378, 2382
C1	4-4-2	(2)	4424, 4447
C2	4-4-2	(2)	3984, 3986
C6	4-4-2	(5)	532, 698, 702, 1680, 1792
C7	4-4-2	(20)	706, 716, 717, 719, 728, 737, 2163, 2164, 2166, 2167, 2168, 2169, 2170, 2172, 2195, 2198, 2199, 2204, 2206, 2208
D2	4-4-0	(5)	4180, 4386, 4387, 4390, 4398
D20	4-4-0	(11)	707, 711, 713, 1207, 1232, 1260, 1665, 2018, 2021, 2022, 2101
D49	4-4-0	(8)	232 *The Badsworth*, 235 *The Bedale*, 247 *The Blankney*, 255 *The Braes of Derwent*, 256 *Hertfordshire*, 269 *The Cleveland*, 336 *The Quorn*, 352 *The Meynell*
F8	2-4-2T	(1)	1581
G5	0-4-4T	(1)	381
J21	0-6-0	(4)	34, 1516, 1807, 1809
J23	0-6-0	(4)	2471, 2472, 2516, 2518
J24	0-6-0	(9)	1821, 1823, 1842, 1844, 1850, 1942, 1951, 1952, 1956

Below: **Raven Class Z Atlantic at York shed c1920.**
Author's collection

Above: **LNER No 2402** *City of York*, **the first of the 1924 batch of Raven Pacifics.** *BR*

J25	0-6-0	(1)	2060
J26	0-6-0	(5)	412, 525, 554, 818, 1130
J27	0-6-0	(6)	2352, 2353, 2355, 2383, 2386, 2392
J39	0-6-0	(2)	1470, 1487
J71	0-6-0T	(13)	237, 296, 347, 399, 447, 495, 499, 1084, 1134, 1140, 1155, 1167, 1758
J72	0-6-0T	(10)	500, 1746, 2182, 2313, 2319, 2328, 2331, 2332, 2333, 2334
J77	0-6-0T	(8)	138, 290, 999, 1000, 1313, 1346, 1348, 1431
J78	0-6-0CT	(1)	590
K3	2-6-0	(12)	17, 28, 39, 52, 53, 1300, 1312, 1318, 1395, 1396, 1397, 1398
N12	0-6-2T	(1)	2485
Q6	0-8-0	(1)	2228
Q7	0-8-0	(1)	628
X3	2-2-4T	(1)	190

Total 165

Service Stock

Engineer's Yard

Y1	0-4-0T	(1) 45	

York Locomotive Allocation 15 March 1943

A1	4-6-2	(5)	2569 *Gladiateur*, 2570 *Tranquil*, 2572 *St Gatien*, 2576 *The White Knight*, 2577 *Night Hawk*.

A7	4-6-2T	(5)	1126, 1176, 1180, 1183, 1193
B16	4-6-0	(69)	840, 841, 842, 843, 844, 845, 846, 847, 848, 849, 906, 908, 909, 911, 914, 915, 920, 921, 922, 923, 924, 926, 927, 928, 929, 930, 931, 932, 933, 934, 936, 937, 942, 943, 1371, 1372, 1373, 1374, 1375, 1376, 1377, 1378, 1379, 1380, 1381, 1382, 1383, 1384, 1385, 2363, 2364, 2365, 2366, 2367, 2368, 2369, 2370, 2371, 2372, 2373, 2374, 2375, 2376, 2377, 2378, 2379, 2380, 2381, 2382
C1	4-4-2	(2)	4424, 4447
C7	4-4-2	(10)	706, 717, 719, 720, 728, 732, 737, 2163, 2164, 2166
D20	4-4-0	(4)	708, 725, 1260, 2027
D49	4-4-0	(13)	205 *The Albrighton*, 222 *The Berkeley*, 226 *The Bilsdale*, 235 *The Bedale*, 255 *The Braes of Derwent*, 258 *The Cattistock*, 274 *The Craven*, 279 *The Cotswold*, 288 *The Percy*, 298 *The Pytchley*, 352 *The Meynell*, 353 *The Derwent*, 359 *The Fitzwilliam*
J21	0-6-0	(13)	300, 470, 778, 806, 871, 965, 997, 1315, 1514, 1555, 1573, 1596, 1615
J71	0-6-0T	(14)	165, 237, 239, 449, 482, 495, 499, 972, 1085, 1134, 1140, 1167, 1196, 1836
J72	0-6-0T	(11)	500, 1728, 1746, 2178, 2182, 2308, 2315, 2319, 2328, 2332, 2334
J77	0-6-0T	(9)	138, 290, 998, 1000, 1313, 1346, 1348, 1349, 1431

Above: **Another engine with York connections! 'D49' No 211** *The York and Ainsty,* **standing at No 5 platform (later No 9).** *Real Photographs*

V2	2 6 2	(20)	3643, 3648, 3656, 3660, 3661, 3666, 3672, 3673, 3674, 4808 *The Green Howards, Alexandra, Princess of Wales's Own Yorkshire Regiment,* 4810, 4814, 4818 *St Peter's School, York,* AD 627, 4827, 4835, 4872, 4875, 4878, 4889, 4896
Y8	0-4-0T	(1)	559
D(SR)	4-4-0	(2)	Southern Railway 2051, 2068

Total 178

Service Stock

Engineer's Yard

Y1	0-4-0T	(1)	45

York Locomotive Allocation 2 October 1954

A1	4-6-2	(5)	60121 *Silurian,* 60138 *Boswell,* 60140 *Balmoral,* 60146 *Peregrine,* 60153 *Flamboyant*
A2/2	4-6-2	(3)	60501 *Cock o' the North,* 60502 *Earl Marischal,* 60503 *Lord President*
A2/3	4-6-2	(4)	6)512 *Steady Aim,* 60515 *Sun Stream,* 60522 *Straight Deal,* 69524 *Herringbone*
A2	4-6-2	(1)	60526 *Sugar Palm*
B1	4-6-0	(15)	61002 *Impala,* 61015 *Duiker,* 61016 *Inyala,* 61020 *Gemsbok,* 61038 *Blacktail,* 61053, 61071, 61084, 61115, 61176, 61224, 61288, 61337, 61338, 61339
B16	4-6-0	(46)	61416, 61417, 61418, 61419, 61420, 61421, 61423, 61424, 61426, 61430, 61434, 61435, 61436, 61437, 61438, 61439, 61441, 61443, 61444, 61446, 61449, 61450, 61451, 61452, 61453, 61454, 61455, 61456, 61457, 61458, 61459, 61460, 61461, 61462, 61463, 61464, 61465, 61466, 61467, 61468, 61472, 61473, 61474, 61475, 61476, 61477
D20	4-4-0	(2)	62343, 62345
D49	4-4-0	(7)	62702 *Oxfordshire,* 62730 *Berkshire,* 62731 *Selkirkshire,* 62745 *The Hurworth,* 62759 *The Craven,* 62760 *The Cotswold,* 62774 *The Staintondale*
J25	0-6-0	(6)	65650, 65654, 65677, 65687, 65691, 65700

J27	0-6-0	(10)	65827, 65844, 65845, 65848, 65849, 65874, 65883, 65887, 65890, 65894
J71	0-6-0T	(10)	68230, 68240, 68246, 68250, 68253, 68275, 68280, 68293, 68297, 68313
J72	0-6-0T	(10)	68677, 68695, 68699, 68722, 68724, 68726, 68735, 68739, 68745, 69020
J77	0-6-0T	(1)	68435
J94	0-6-0T	(9)	68029, 68031, 68032, 68040, 68042, 68044, 68046, 68051, 68061
V2	2-6-2	(30)	60837, 60839, 60843, 60847 *St Peter's School, York, AD 627*, 60856, 60864, 60895, 60901, 60904, 60907, 60918, 60925, 60929, 60934, 60941, 60946, 60954, 60960, 60961, 60962, 60963, 60968, 60974, 60975, 60976, 60977, 60978, 60979, 60981, 60982
WD	2-8-0	(10)	90044, 90047, 90056, 90100, 90200, 90424, 90500, 90517, 90518, 90603

Total 169

Service Stock

Motive Power Depot

Y8	0-4-0T	(1)	55

Engineer's Yard

Y1	0-4-0T	(1)	53

Below: **The 'V2' named after** *St Peter's School York AD627.* BR

York Locomotive Allocation 11 January 1964

Steam

4MT	2-6-0	(4)	43055, 43071, 43097, 43126
A1	4-6-2	(13)	60120 *Kittiwake*, 60121 *Silurian*, 60124 *Kenilworth*, 60126 *Sir Vincent Raven*, 60138 *Boswell*, 60140 *Balmoral*, 60141 *Abbotsford*, 60143 *Sir Walter Scott*, 60145 *Saint Mungo*, 60146 *Peregrine*, 60147 *North Eastern*, 60150 *Willbrook*, 60155 *Borderer*
B1	4-6-0	(11)	61002 *Impala*, 61018 *Gnu*, 61021 *Reitbok*, 61031 *Reedbuck*, 61049, 61062, 61084, 61198, 61275, 61276, 61337
B16	4-6-0	(5)	61421, 61434, 61448, 61454, 61457
J27	0-6-0	(2)	65844, 65894
K1	2-6-0	(18)	62005, 62007, 62009, 62010, 62028, 62029, 62042, 62046, 62047, 62049, 62056, 62057, 62058, 62060, 62061, 62062, 62063, 62065,
V2	2-6-2	(26)	60810, 60828, 60831, 60833, 60837, 60847 *St Peter's School, York, AD 627*, 60855, 60856, 60864, 60876, 60877, 60886, 60887, 60895, 60925, 60929, 60932, 60939, 60941, 60942, 60945, 60961, 60963, 60967, 60975, 60982
WD	2-8-0	(7)	90030, 90045, 90078, 90217, 90517, 90518, 90663
9F	2-10-0	(8)	92005, 92006, 92205, 92206, 92011, 92021, 92031, 92039

Above: **No D5096 at York South shed. The building in the background is the old Great North of England shed but re-roofed.** *E. Sanderson*

Diesel

20/3	1C-C1	(3)	D252, D253, D254, D258, D259, D275, D276, D278, D281, D282, D283, D284, D285, D345, D346, D347, D348, D349, D350, D351, D352, D353, D354, D355, D356, D357, D385, D386, D387, D388, D389, D390, D391
2/1	0-6-0	(15)	D2046, D2051, D2062, D2063, D2065, D2066, D2075, D2111, D2112, D2113, D2151, D2158, D2159, D2160, D2161
2/13	0-6-0	(4)	D2245, D2268, D2269, D2270
3/1	0-6-0	(15)	D3070, D3071, D3076, D3237, D3238, D3239, D3240, D3313, D3314, D3315, D3319, D3320, D3872, D3874, D3946
11/1A	Bo-Bo	(4)	D5096, D5098, D5099, D5100
12/1	Bo-Bo	(1)	D5176

Total 166

York Locomotive Allocation 1 January 1971

40	(17)	250, 251, 252, 253, 254, 256, 257, 258, 259, 272, 274, 275, 276, 277, 278, 279, 281
47	(18)	1100, 1107, 1513, 1514, 1515, 1516, 1517, 1518, 1519, 1533, 1541, 1542, 1543, 1570, 1571, 1572, 1573, 1574
03	(7)	2054, 2063, 2073, 2075, 2101, 2113, 2150
08	(11)	3076, 3237, 3238, 3239, 3240, 3315, 3319, 3726, 3872, 3874, 4044
20	(11)	8024, 8300, 8301, 8302, 8303, 8304, 8305, 8306, 8307, 8308, 8309

Total 64

York Locomotive Allocation, 3 January 1982

The 37 locomotives transferred away when York shed closed on this date were:

To Tinsley
31.141/171/218/220/222/272/327 (7)

To Immingham
31.142/162/168/175/186/188/196/402/403/404/405/406/407/408/409/411 (16)

To Gateshead
47.423/425/426/428/429/430/431/457/458/520/525/526/527/528 (14)

In the two preceding weeks the last 'Deltic' locomotives were withdrawn from York:

55.013	20 December 1981
55.010	24 December 1981
55.016	30 December 1981
55.007/008/017/019/021	31 December 1981
55.002/009/015/022	2 January 1982